The College Panda

ACT Math
Workbook

More Advanced Practice By Topic

ISBN: 978-0-9894964-8-3

*ACT is a registered trademark of ACT, Inc., which does not endorse this product.

For more information, visit thecollegepanda.com

Discounts available for teachers and companies. Please contact thecollegepanda@gmail.com for details.

Table of Contents

1

Absolute Value

Answers start on page 89.

1. $-4\left|-11+5\right| = ?$

   A. -64
   B. -24
   C. -10
   D. 24
   E. 64

2. If $x \leq -3$, then $|x+3| = ?$

   A. $x-3$
   B. $x+3$
   C. $-x-3$
   D. $-x+3$
   E. 0

3. What is the value of $(x-y)^2 - |x-y|$ when $x=5$ and $y=7$?

   A. -4
   B. -2
   C. 2
   D. 4
   E. 6

4. If $|5-y| = 10$, what are the possible values for y?

   A. -10 and 5
   B. -10 and 15
   C. -5 and 10
   D. -5 and 15
   E. 10 and 15

5. Which of the following is equivalent to $|x-3|$ for all real values of x?

   A. $x-3$
   B. $3-x$
   C. $|-x-3|$
   D. $|3-x|$
   E. $|x+3|$

6. For all real numbers x, $|x|^2$ is equivalent to all of the following EXCEPT:

   A. $(-x)^2$
   B. $|-x|^2$
   C. $|-x^2|$
   D. $-x^2$
   E. x^2

7. For all real numbers y, the value of $|y| - y$ is:

   A. always zero.
   B. sometimes positive.
   C. always positive.
   D. sometimes negative.
   E. always negative.

8. If $x < y$, then $|x-y| = ?$

   A. $-x-y$
   B. $x-y$
   C. $x+y$
   D. $y-x$
   E. xy

5

9. For all real numbers x, $|x - 3| + |3 - x| = ?$

    A. $2(x - 3)$

    B. $2|x - 3|$

    C. 0

    D. $2(x + 3)$

    E. $2|x + 3|$

2

Exponents & Radicals

Answers start on page 90.

1. $\dfrac{6x^8}{3x^2}$ is equivalent to:

   A. $\dfrac{2}{x^4}$

   B. $2x^4$

   C. $2x^6$

   D. $3x^3$

   E. $3x^6$

2. For positive values of x, which of the following is equivalent to $x^{\frac{3}{2}}$?

   A. $1.5x$

   B. $\dfrac{x^3}{2}$

   C. $x\sqrt{x}$

   D. $\left(\dfrac{x}{2}\right)^3$

   E. $\sqrt[3]{x^2}$

3. What is the value of $x^3 + x^2$ when $x = -2$?

   A. -12

   B. -4

   C. -2

   D. 4

   E. 12

4. Which of the following is equivalent to $(x+1)^0$ whenever $x \neq -1$?

   A. $x+1$

   B. 0

   C. 1

   D. 2

   E. 3

5. $3n^{-2} \cdot 2n^{-3}$ is equivalent to:

   A. $-6n^5$

   B. $5n^6$

   C. $6n^6$

   D. $\dfrac{6}{n^5}$

   E. $\dfrac{6}{n^6}$

6. For nonzero values of x and y, which of the following expressions is equivalent to $-\dfrac{20x^8y^4}{5x^2y}$?

   A. $-4x^4y^4$

   B. $-4x^6y^3$

   C. $-4x^6y^4$

   D. $-15x^6y^3$

   E. $-25x^6y^3$

7. When x, y, and z are real numbers and $x^2 y^3 z^4 > 0$, which of the following *must* be greater than 0?

   A. xz
   B. xy
   C. xyz
   D. $x^2 y$
   E. yz

8. For what real number value of b is the equation $(x^3)^4 (x^2)^5 = (x^b)^2$ true?

   A. 7
   B. 11
   C. 14
   D. 22
   E. 60

9. What is the value of $\sqrt{a^2 - b^2}$ when $a = \sqrt{23}$ and $b = \sqrt{5}$?

   A. $\sqrt{28}$
   B. $3\sqrt{2}$
   C. $4\sqrt{3}$
   D. $6\sqrt{14}$
   E. 18

10. $2(a^3)^2 \cdot (2a^3)^2$ is equivalent to:

   A. $8a^{10}$
   B. $8a^{12}$
   C. $16a^{10}$
   D. $16a^{12}$
   E. $16a^{36}$

11. If $a > 0$, $\sqrt{\dfrac{a}{2}} + \sqrt{\dfrac{2}{a}}$ is equivalent to which of the following?

   A. 1
   B. $\dfrac{2\sqrt{2a}}{a + 2}$
   C. $2\sqrt{2a}$
   D. $\dfrac{a + 2}{2a}$
   E. $\dfrac{a + 2}{\sqrt{2a}}$

12. Given that j, k, and x are positive integers, which of the following statements is true whenever $x^{3j} = (-x)^k$?

   A. $k = \dfrac{j}{3}$ and k is odd
   B. $k = j$ and k is even
   C. $k = j$ and k is odd
   D. $k = 3j$ and k is even
   E. $k = 3j$ and k is odd

3

Manipulating and Solving Equations

Answers start on page 91.

1. If $\dfrac{b}{-3} - 2 = -10$, then $b = ?$

    A. -36
    B. -24
    C. 4
    D. 24
    E. 36

2. The only solution to the equation $(x - 11)(x - 3) = a$ is $x = 8$. What is a ?

    A. -15
    B. -14
    C. 14
    D. 15
    E. 28

3. Whenever $x^2 y = 4$ for positive values of x and y, which of the following equations gives x in terms of y ?

    A. $x = 4y^2$
    B. $x = \sqrt{2y}$
    C. $x = \dfrac{2}{y}$
    D. $x = \dfrac{2}{\sqrt{y}}$
    E. $x = \dfrac{4}{y^2}$

4. What is the solution to the equation $\dfrac{1}{3}(2x + 1) = \dfrac{1}{2}(x - 4)$?

    A. -14
    B. -10
    C. -2
    D. 6
    E. 12

5.

$$d = a\left(\frac{c+1}{24}\right)$$

Doctors use Cowling's rule, shown above, to determine the right dosage d, in milligrams, of medication for a child based on the adult dosage a, in milligrams, and the child's age c, in years. Which of the following expressions gives c when the adult dosage is 6 milligrams?

A. $\frac{d}{4} - 1$

B. $\frac{d}{4} + 1$

C. $\frac{d-1}{4}$

D. $4d - 1$

E. $4d + 1$

6. For the equation $\frac{b}{a+1} = c$, which of the following expressions gives a in terms of b and c?

A. $\frac{b}{c} - 1$

B. $\frac{b-1}{c}$

C. $\frac{c}{b} - 1$

D. $\frac{c}{b} + 1$

E. $bc + 1$

7. If $2ax = 3 - bx$, which of the following equations gives x in terms of a and b?

A. $\frac{3-b}{2a}$

B. $\frac{3-2a}{b}$

C. $\frac{3}{2a+b}$

D. $3 - 2ab$

E. $3 - 2a - b$

8. If $ab = ac + bc$, which of the following equations gives b in terms of a and c?

A. $\frac{ac}{a+c}$

B. $\frac{ac}{a-c}$

C. $\frac{a-c}{ac}$

D. $c + \frac{c}{a}$

E. $ac + c - a$

9. The total dollar amount in a bank account can be modeled by the formula $A = A_0(1+i)^t$, where A_0 is the initial deposit, in dollars; i is the annual interest rate, expressed as a decimal; and A is the dollar amount in the account after t years. Which of the following equations shows the formula solved for i?

A. $i = \sqrt[t]{\frac{A}{A_0} + 1}$

B. $i = \sqrt[t]{\frac{A}{A_0}} + 1$

C. $i = \sqrt[t]{\frac{A}{A_0}} - 1$

D. $i = \sqrt[t]{\frac{A}{A_0} - 1}$

E. $i = t\log\left(\frac{A}{A_0}\right) - 1$

10. Given that $a, b, c,$ and d are real numbers that satisfy $b = a^2, c = \sqrt{d},$ and $b = d$, which of the following equations is NOT necessarily true?

A. $c = \sqrt{b}$

B. $a = c$

C. $b^2 = d^2$

D. $d = a^2$

E. $d = c^2$

Expressions

Answers start on page 93.

1. The expression $b^2 - 8b + 16$ is equivalent to:

   A. $(b+4)^2$
   B. $(b-4)^2$
   C. $(b+4)(b-4)$
   D. $(b-8)(b-2)$
   E. $(b-8)(b+2)$

2. Which of the following is a simplified form of the expression $a(b+c) + b(a+c) + c(a+b)$?

   A. $3abc$
   B. $6abc$
   C. $2a + 2b + 2c$
   D. $2ab + 2bc + 2ac$
   E. $3ab + 3bc + 3ac$

3. Which of the following expressions is equivalent to $-x^2y - xy^2$?

   A. $-xy(x+y)$
   B. $-xy(x-y)$
   C. $-xy(y-x)$
   D. $xy(x+y)$
   E. $xy(x-y)$

4. $(3a - 4b)(5b + 2a)$ is equivalent to:

   A. $6ab$
   B. $23ab$
   C. $6a^2 + 7ab - 20b^2$
   D. $6a^2 + 23ab - 20b^2$
   E. $-7a^2b^2$

5. It takes 4 cups of water to make 3 pizzas. It takes 5 cups of water to make 4 cakes. Which of the following expressions gives the number of cups of water needed to make x pizzas and y cakes?

   A. $4x + 5y$
   B. $12x + 20y$
   C. $\dfrac{3}{4}x + \dfrac{4}{5}y$
   D. $\dfrac{4}{3}x + \dfrac{4}{5}y$
   E. $\dfrac{4}{3}x + \dfrac{5}{4}y$

6. Which of the following expressions is equivalent to $4x^2 + 2x - 6$?

   A. $(4x + 1)(x - 6)$
   B. $(4x - 1)(x + 6)$
   C. $2(x - 1)(2x + 3)$
   D. $2(x + 1)(2x - 3)$
   E. $2(2x - 1)(x + 3)$

7. The expression $(x + 2)^2 - 4x - 5$ is equivalent to:

   A. $x^2 - 5$
   B. $x^2 + 1$
   C. $x^2 - 4x - 1$
   D. $(x + 1)(x - 1)$
   E. $(x - 4)(x - 1)$

8. For $x^2 \neq 16$, $\dfrac{(x+4)^2}{x^2-16} = ?$

   A. $\dfrac{x+4}{x-4}$

   B. $\dfrac{1}{x+4}$

   C. $\dfrac{1}{x-4}$

   D. $-\dfrac{1}{4}$

   E. $\dfrac{1}{4}$

9. Which of the following is the least common denominator for $\dfrac{1}{3x-6} + \dfrac{1}{2(x-2)^2}$?

   A. $(x-2)$
   B. $(x-2)^2$
   C. $6(x-2)$
   D. $6(x-2)^2$
   E. $6(x-2)^3$

10. At Jack's Burger Shack, Michael orders x burgers with y additional condiments on each burger. Each burger cost b dollars and each additional condiment cost c dollars. If Michael paid less than \$30 for his order, which of the following expressions represents the amount of money, in dollars, that Michael should have received back after he paid for his order with \$30?
    (Note: There is no tax on food at Jack's Burger Shack.)

    A. $bx + cy$
    B. $bx + cxy$
    C. $30 - (bx + cy)$
    D. $30 - (bx - cxy)$
    E. $30 - (bx + cxy)$

5

Numbers and Operations

Answers start on page 94.

1. When David divides m by 12, he gets $\frac{1}{4}$. When Adam multiples m by 12, what number does he get?

    A. 3
    B. 4
    C. 6
    D. 24
    E. 36

2. Jared fills each of ten jars with at least one jellybean. Each jar contains a different number of jellybeans, except for two jars which contain the same number of jellybeans. What is the minimum total number of jellybeans that Jared could have put into the jars?

    A. 45
    B. 46
    C. 47
    D. 48
    E. 49

3. For every three boxes of chocolate bought at the regular price of $20 each, a fourth can be bought for $10. If Jake bought 11 boxes of chocolate and paid the least amount of money possible, how much did he pay?

    A. $180
    B. $190
    C. $200
    D. $210
    E. $220

4. Which of the following gives the range of numbers that are within $\frac{4}{3}$ of the number 0.75?

    A. $-\frac{25}{12}$ to $\frac{7}{12}$
    B. $-\frac{25}{12}$ to $\frac{25}{12}$
    C. $-\frac{7}{12}$ to $\frac{25}{12}$
    D. $-\frac{7}{12}$ to $\frac{7}{12}$
    E. -2 to 2

5. The expression $\dfrac{2-\dfrac{1}{6}}{1-\dfrac{1}{12}}$ is equal to:

   A. $\dfrac{1}{2}$

   B. 1

   C. 2

   D. 3

   E. $\dfrac{121}{72}$

6. Martin has $8.00 in quarters to spend on doing laundry. If the laundry machine cost $1.25 per load, how many quarters will Martin have left after doing 3 loads of laundry?
   (Note: Each quarter is worth $0.25.)

   A. 14
   B. 15
   C. 16
   D. 17
   E. 18

7. Lia rented a car for a fixed fee of $60, plus $1.50 for every mile she traveled. When she returned the car, Lia was told the total bill was $113. However, she had recorded the distance of her trip and thought the bill was $20 more than it should have been. If Lia was correct, how many miles did she travel using her rental car?

   A. 19
   B. 22
   C. 25
   D. 28
   E. 31

8. A chef has $5\dfrac{3}{4}$ cups of olive oil in the kitchen. Each pizza he makes requires $\dfrac{2}{3}$ cup of olive oil. Which of the following is the maximum number of whole pizzas for which he has enough olive oil?

   A. 7
   B. 8
   C. 9
   D. 10
   E. 11

9. Which of the following operations will produce the smallest result when substituted for the blank in the expression 28_____(-2) ?

   A. Minus
   B. Plus
   C. Divided by
   D. Multiplied by
   E. Raised to the power of

10. Jane had 6 pizzas delivered to her house for $50.88, which included a delivery surcharge of $8.28. At the same per-pizza cost, what is the cost of an order of 8 pizzas before the delivery surcharge is added?

    A. $7.10
    B. $8.48
    C. $56.80
    D. $67.84
    E. $78.88

11. For physics class, Alistair must complete an assigned exercise set in 10 days. He completes $\dfrac{3}{20}$ of the exercise set each of the first 4 days. For the remaining 6 days, what fraction of the entire exercise set, on average, must Alistair complete per day?

    A. $\dfrac{2}{5}$

    B. $\dfrac{3}{5}$

    C. $\dfrac{3}{10}$

    D. $\dfrac{1}{15}$

    E. $\dfrac{1}{20}$

6

Properties of Numbers

Answers start on page 95.

1. There are 20 cards in a bowl and on each card is a different number from 1 to 20. Jamie and Elizabeth each pick out 5 cards. Two of Jamie's cards are 16 and 19. Two of Elizabeth's cards are 6 and 17. What is the largest sum that Elizabeth's cards can have?

   A. 68
   B. 70
   C. 76
   D. 77
   E. 80

2. If 14 is subtracted from the sum of $3x$ and $4x$, and x is an integer, the result must be a multiple of

   A. 2
   B. 3
   C. 5
   D. 7
   E. 11

3. Which of the following numbers is divisible by 9 and 5, but not by 6?

   A. 540
   B. 550
   C. 585
   D. 625
   E. 630

4. The square root of a given number is approximately 7.4162. The given number is between what 2 integers?

   A. 2 and 3
   B. 4 and 9
   C. 16 and 24
   D. 25 and 36
   E. 49 and 64

5. What is the smallest 3-digit integer that has a factor of 6 and is a multiple of 7?

   A. 105
   B. 114
   C. 121
   D. 126
   E. 168

6. The diameter of Star X, which is 8.1×10^9 miles, is approximately how many times the diameter of Star Y, which is 2.6×10^4 miles?

   A. 3×10^5
   B. 6×10^5
   C. 3×10^{13}
   D. 1×10^{14}
   E. 2×10^{14}

7. On the real number line, -0.0728 is between $\dfrac{n}{100}$ and $\dfrac{(n+1)}{100}$ for some integer n. What is the value of n ?

   A. -728
   B. -73
   C. -72
   D. -8
   E. -7

8. For what values of y is the expression $\dfrac{1}{9-y^2}$ undefined?

   A. -9 and 9
   B. -3 and 3
   C. -1 and 1
   D. $-\dfrac{1}{3}$ and $\dfrac{1}{3}$
   E. $-\dfrac{1}{9}$ and $\dfrac{1}{9}$

9. The product of the first 50 positive integers is divided by the product of the first 49 positive integers. What is the result?

   A. 2
   B. 49
   C. 50
   D. 99
   E. 2,450

10. A face-down card has a single digit written on it. Three of the following statements are true, and the other is false:

   I.   The digit is 4
   II. The digit is not 5
   III. The digit is 6
   IV. The digit is even

   Which of the following must be true?

   A. I is true
   B. II is false
   C. III is true
   D. III is false
   E. IV is true

11.

| 21 | 63 | 10 | 82 | 46 |

Four numbers are selected from the five numbers shown on the cards above. The units digit of the sum of the four selected numbers is 0. What is the number that was not selected?

   A. 10
   B. 21
   C. 46
   D. 63
   E. 82

12. The number 6 has four different factors: 1, 2, 3, and 6. How many positive integers less than 30 have exactly four different factors?

   A. 7
   B. 8
   C. 9
   D. 10
   E. 11

13. The number 204 is written as the product of two positive integers A and B such that the difference between A and B is as small as possible. What is the difference between A and B ?

   A. 3
   B. 5
   C. 28
   D. 47
   E. 65

14. The 3 statements given below are all true about certain positive integers $a, b,$ and c.

   1. a is a prime number such that $10 < a < 20$
   2. b is a perfect square such that $1 < b < 10$
   3. c is a multiple of 6 such that $10 < c < 20$

   What is the minimum possible value of $\dfrac{ab}{c}$?

   A. $\dfrac{22}{9}$

   B. $\dfrac{26}{9}$

   C. $\dfrac{11}{3}$

   D. $\dfrac{19}{2}$

   E. $\dfrac{57}{4}$

15. If the square of x is equal to 8, which of the following statements about x *must* be true?

   A. x is positive
   B. x is even
   C. x is rational
   D. x is irrational
   E. x is imaginary

7
Complex Numbers

Answers start on page 97.

1. The *absolute value* of a complex number $a + bi$, where a and b are real numbers and $i^2 = -1$, is defined by $\sqrt{a^2 + b^2}$. The absolute value of $-2 + 3i$ is:

   A. i
   B. $5i$
   C. $i\sqrt{5}$
   D. $\sqrt{5}$
   E. $\sqrt{13}$

2. The solution set for which of the following equations contains 0, $-i$ and i ?

   A. $x^2 - 1 = 0$
   B. $x^2 + 1 = 0$
   C. $x(x^2 - 1) = 0$
   D. $x(x^2 + 1) = 0$
   E. $x^2(x + 1) = 0$

3. The product of the complex number $3 - 4i$ and another number is 25. What is the other number?

   A. $-4 + 3i$
   B. $\dfrac{3}{25} - \dfrac{4}{25}i$
   C. $3 + 4i$
   D. $22 + 4i$
   E. $75 - 100i$

4. For $i^2 = -1$, $(3 - i)^2 = ?$

   A. 8
   B. 10
   C. $8 - 3i$
   D. $8 - 6i$
   E. $10 - 6i$

5. The solution set for the equation $\sqrt{x^2 + 9} = 1$ contains:

   A. 1 imaginary number only.
   B. 2 imaginary numbers.
   C. 1 negative real number only.
   D. 2 positive real numbers.
   E. 1 positive and 1 negative real number.

6. The sum of 2 numbers is $10i$, where $i^2 = -1$. If 1 of the numbers is the complex number $5 + 3i$, what is the other number?

   A. $-30 + 50i$
   B. $-5 + 7i$
   C. $5 - 7i$
   D. $5 - 3i$
   E. $2i$

7. Which of the following gives the complex number solutions to the equation $2x^2 + 7 = -11$?

   A. $\pm 3i$

   B. $\pm 6i$

   C. $\pm 9i$

   D. $\pm 12i$

   E. $\pm 18i$

8. Which of the following complex numbers equals $(-2 - i)(5 + 7i)$?

   A. $3 + 6i$

   B. -3

   C. $-3 - 19i$

   D. $-10 - 26i$

   E. $-17 - 19i$

9. A quadratic equation has solutions $x = a \pm \sqrt{-4b^2}$, where a and b are positive real numbers. Which of the following expressions gives these solutions as complex numbers?

   A. $a \pm 2bi$

   B. $a \pm 2b^2 i$

   C. $a \pm 4bi$

   D. $a \pm 4b^2 i$

   E. $a \pm 8bi$

10. Which of the following complex numbers is equal to $\dfrac{4 - 3i}{2 + i}$?

    A. $\dfrac{5}{3} - \dfrac{10}{3}i$

    B. $\dfrac{11}{5} - 2i$

    C. $1 - 10i$

    D. $1 - 2i$

    E. $2 - 4i$

8
Rates

Answers start on page 98.

1. A grocery store sells avocados at 5 for $4.80. At this price, how much would the grocery store charge for 3 avocados?

   A. $2.61
   B. $2.76
   C. $2.88
   D. $3.12
   E. $3.52

2. Greg runs laps around the school track every week. When he first started, he could run 10 laps in 45 minutes. Now he can run 12 laps in 30 minutes. By how many minutes has he improved his average lap time?

   A. 1.5
   B. 2
   C. 2.5
   D. 3
   E. 3.5

3. A cricket moves at a constant rate of 14 feet every 3 minutes. At this rate, which of the following is closest to the number of *inches* the cricket moves in 30 *seconds*?

   A. 21
   B. 24
   C. 26
   D. 28
   E. 35

4. How many minutes would it take a bus to travel 30 kilometers at a constant speed of 40 kilometers per hour?

   A. 30
   B. 40
   C. 45
   D. 60
   E. 75

5. Fred starts with a certain number of stamps in his stamp collection. Every 2 days he adds 5 new stamps to his collection. At the end of 8 days there are 90 stamps in his collection. How many stamps does Fred have in his collection at the end of 40 days?

   A. 170
   B. 180
   C. 190
   D. 200
   E. 250

6. Albert, Henry, and Nelson each drink three cups of home brewed coffee each day. Judy drinks only two. They have enough coffee beans to last 24 days. If Judy starts drinking three cups a day, instead of two, how many days will their supply of coffee beans last?

   A. 19
   B. 20
   C. 21
   D. 22
   E. 23

7. At Al's Printing Center, the cost of making copies is $0.20 per page. If Kate decides to copy a 20,000-word document that has an average of 800 words on each page, how much will she have to pay at Al's Printing Center?

   A. $4.80
   B. $5.00
   C. $5.20
   D. $5.40
   E. $5.60

8. Roommates Adam and Billy both needed to ship packages at a post office 3 miles from their house. Adam rode his bicycle to the post office at a constant speed of 10 miles per hour. Billy walked to the post office at a constant speed of 4 miles per hour. If they left their house at the same time, Adam arrived at the post office how many minutes before Billy?

   A. 18
   B. 27
   C. 32
   D. 36
   E. 45

9. Joey starts to run a track that is 4 miles long. He alternates running one-quarter mile at 10 miles per hour, and then walking one-half mile at 5 miles per hour. How many minutes does it take him to complete the track?

   A. 32
   B. 35
   C. 37
   D. 39
   E. 41

10. Zane lives 1 mile away from school. To get to school on time, he leaves home at 7:30 AM everyday and walks at a steady speed of 4 miles per hour. Today he felt particularly tired and walked the first $\frac{1}{2}$ mile at a speed of only 3 miles per hour. At how many miles per hour must Zane run the last $\frac{1}{2}$ mile to arrive at school on time?

   A. 5
   B. 5.5
   C. 6
   D. 6.5
   E. 8

9

Ratio & Proportion

Answers start on page 99.

1. Mark, the owner of a men's shoe store, surveyed a number of customers for their shoe sizes. The results are given in the table below.

Shoe size	Number of customers
9	10
10	31
11	22
12	12

Mark will order 300 shoes in the proportions, by shoe size, in the table. How many size-10 shoes will he order?

A. 40
B. 48
C. 88
D. 93
E. 124

2. A juice recipe calls for 5 cups of blueberries and 2 cups of water. Jacob puts x cups of blueberries into his blender. Which of the following expressions gives the number of cups of water he should add to maintain the ratio of blueberries to water in this juice recipe?

A. $\frac{2}{7}x$

B. $\frac{2}{5}x$

C. $\frac{5}{7}x$

D. $\frac{5}{2}x$

E. $\frac{7}{2}x$

3. The lengths of the 3 sides of a triangle are in the ratio 4:5:7. The perimeter of the triangle is 112 cm. What is the length, in cm, of the shortest side of the triangle?

A. 7
B. 28
C. 35
D. 42
E. 49

4. The table below gives estimated values for variables x and y. Researchers believe that y is directly proportional to x. Based on the estimated data, which of the following values best approximates the constant of variation? (Note: The variable y is directly proportional to the variable x if $y = kx$ for some nonzero constant, k, called the *constant of variation*.)

x	y
4.42	16.68
5.61	21.14
8.25	31.18
10.44	39.55
12.74	48.22

  A. 0.25
  B. 3.80
  C. 4.15
  D. 12.25
  E. 73.75

5. Which of the following proportions, when solved for x, gives the correct answer to the problem given below?

    Find the value of x that equals 78% of 40.

  A. $\dfrac{40}{78} = \dfrac{x}{100}$

  B. $\dfrac{40}{100} = \dfrac{78}{x}$

  C. $\dfrac{78}{x} = \dfrac{x}{40}$

  D. $\dfrac{78}{100} = \dfrac{x}{40}$

  E. $\dfrac{78}{100} = \dfrac{40}{x}$

6. The ratio of x to y is 3 to 2, and the ratio of y to z is 1 to 2. What is the value of $\dfrac{2x + y}{y + 2z}$?

  A. $\dfrac{3}{5}$

  B. $\dfrac{4}{5}$

  C. $\dfrac{7}{8}$

  D. 1

  E. $\dfrac{8}{5}$

7. The lengths of the sides of a right triangle are in the ratio of 3:4:5. The area of the triangle is 108 square inches. How many inches long is the hypotenuse of the triangle?

  A. 15
  B. $15\sqrt{2}$
  C. 20
  D. $20\sqrt{2}$
  E. 25

8. A retail store uses a *demand index* to figure out which products to hold in stock. A product's demand index varies directly as the square root of the product's price in dollars and inversely as the product's weight in pounds. If k represents the constant of variation, which of the following expressions represents the demand index of a product that has a price of p dollars and weighs w pounds?

  A. $\dfrac{k}{w\sqrt{p}}$

  B. $\dfrac{kw}{\sqrt{p}}$

  C. $\dfrac{k\sqrt{p}}{w}$

  D. $\dfrac{w\sqrt{p}}{k}$

  E. $kw\sqrt{p}$

9. For every 3 cans of soda Jimmy drinks, Alice drinks 5 cans. Alice drank 46 more cans of soda than Jimmy did this month. How many cans did Alice drink this month?

  A. 69
  B. 75
  C. 92
  D. 104
  E. 115

10. A bale of hay can feed either 8 horses or 15 ponies. If there are 5 bales of hay and 24 horses, how many ponies can be fed after the horses are fed?

  A. 18
  B. 20
  C. 25
  D. 30
  E. 32

11. Frank uses 3 ounces of raspberry-flavored syrup, 1 ounce of lime juice, and 16 ounces of sparkling water to make raspberry spritzer. There are 40 calories in 1 ounce of raspberry-flavored syrup, 10 calories in 1 ounce of lime juice, and no calories in sparkling water. How many calories are in 60 ounces of Frank's raspberry spritzer?

  A. 130
  B. 150
  C. 360
  D. 370
  E. 390

12. Two particles are 8 centimeters apart. The electric force between them varies inversely with the square of the distance between them. How many centimeters apart would the two particles need to be to have half the electric force between them as they currently have?

  A. $8\sqrt{2}$
  B. 12
  C. $12\sqrt{2}$
  D. 16
  E. 64

10 Percent

Answers start on page 101.

1. The population of Somerville 50 years ago was 80% of what it is today. The population of Somerville today is 84,000. Which of the following is closest to the population of Somerville 50 years ago?

   A. 16,800
   B. 42,000
   C. 67,200
   D. 68,600
   E. 105,000

2. 60% of 210 is equal to 40% of what number?

   A. $50\frac{2}{5}$
   B. $176\frac{2}{5}$
   C. 180
   D. 230
   E. 315

3. The regular price of a jacket is $180.00. The jacket is on sale for 10% off the regular price. A coupon, for today only, gives an additional discount of 15% off the sale price. What is the price of the jacket today with the coupon? (Note: Ignore sales tax.)

   A. $133.30
   B. $135.00
   C. $137.70
   D. $142.00
   E. $155.00

4. If x is 20% of y, then 125% of y is what percent of x ?

   A. 145%
   B. 216%
   C. 270%
   D. 350%
   E. 625%

5. During a sale, a store offers TVs at 30% off the original price. John has a coupon that gives an additional 20% discount on the sale price. If John buys a TV with the coupon, what is the percentage discount he receives on the original price?

   A. 44%
   B. 46%
   C. 50%
   D. 52%
   E. 56%

6. A number is decreased by 40% and the resulting number is then increased by 30%. The final number if what percent of the original number?

   A. 70%
   B. 72%
   C. 75%
   D. 78%
   E. 80%

7. A bottle contains 20 ounces of a drink that is 35% water, 60% pineapple juice, and 5% vanilla syrup. Five ounces of pineapple juice are added to the bottle. What percent of the drink is now pineapple juice?

   A. 68%
   B. 75%
   C. 77%
   D. 84%
   E. 85%

8. Rachel is selling cookies to raise money for her school. She started with 110 chocolate chip cookies and 140 oatmeal cookies. She sold 80% of the chocolate chip cookies and 40% of the oatmeal cookies. If her goal is to sell 70% of the cookies she started with, how many more cookies does she need to sell?

   A. 19
   B. 25
   C. 28
   D. 31
   E. 33

9. A restaurant sells pizza in three different sizes: small, medium, and large. A large pizza costs 40% more than a medium pizza. A small pizza costs 20% less than a medium pizza. The cost of a large pizza is what percent greater than the cost of a small pizza?

   A. 45%
   B. 60%
   C. 65%
   D. 75%
   E. 80%

10. Matt wants to buy a mattress that has a retail price of $800. He is deciding between two stores that have different sales tax policies for discounted products. To get the final price, Store A adds an 8% sales tax to the retail price of the mattress and then discounts the result by 25%. Store B discounts the retail price of the mattress by 25% and then adds an 8% sales tax to the result. Which store, if either, gives Matt the better deal, and by how many dollars?

   A. Store A, $3.24
   B. Store A, $6.48
   C. Store B, $3.24
   D. Store B, $6.48
   E. Matt would pay the same amount at either store.

11

Functions

Answers start on page 102.

1. What is the value of $f(-1)$ when

$$f(x) = \frac{5(x^2 + x - 6)}{x - 2} ?$$

   A. -10
   B. $\dfrac{20}{3}$
   C. 10
   D. 20
   E. 30

2. What is the value of $f(x) = 9 - (-2)^x$ when $x = 3$?

   A. 1
   B. 3
   C. $9\dfrac{1}{8}$
   D. 15
   E. 17

3. The operation ★ is defined as follows:

$$★n = 2n \quad \text{when } n \text{ is odd}$$
$$★n = n + 3 \quad \text{when } n \text{ is even}$$

   What is the value of $★(★5)$?

   A. 7
   B. 10
   C. 13
   D. 16
   E. 53

4. Which of the following values is a zero of $f(x) = 2x^3 + 7x^2 - 4x$?

   A. -5
   B. -4
   C. $-\dfrac{1}{2}$
   D. 2
   E. 3

5. The operation ⊛ is defined by $a ⊛ b = 3a - 2b$. If $6 ⊛ 4 = 8 ⊛ n$, what is the value of n ?

   A. 1
   B. 3
   C. 5
   D. 7
   E. 9

6. If $f(x) = -2x + 3$, then $f(f(2x)) = ?$

   A. $-8x + 9$
   B. $8x + 9$
   C. $8x - 3$
   D. $8x + 3$
   E. $8x^3 - 6x + 3$

7. Which of the following definitions for $f(x)$ yields the greatest value for all $x > 4$?

    A. $f(x) = 2x$

    B. $f(x) = x^2$

    C. $f(x) = 2^x$

    D. $f(x) = \dfrac{2}{x}$

    E. $f(x) = \sqrt{x}$

8. For functions f and g defined by

    $f(x) = \dfrac{1}{2}x + 1$ and $g(x) = 3x - 2$, which of

    the following expressions is equal to $f(g(2m))$?

    A. $3m$

    B. $3m - 1$

    C. $3m + 1$

    D. $6m$

    E. $6m - 1$

9. Consider the function $f(x) = |x| - 5$. What is the value of $f(f(2))$?

    A. -8

    B. -3

    C. -2

    D. 2

    E. 3

Use the following information to answer questions 10–11.

The table below gives the value of $f(x)$ for certain values of x.

x	$f(x)$
-2	5
-1	2
0	-2
1	4
2	3
3	5

10. What is the value of $f^{-1}(2)$?

    A. -1

    B. 0

    C. 3

    D. 4

    E. 5

11. The function $g(x)$ is defined in terms of $f(x)$ by $g(x) = f(x - 5) + 4$. What is the value of $g(3)$?

    A. 4

    B. 6

    C. 7

    D. 8

    E. 9

12. The domain of the function $M(x, y) = x^2 - y^2$ is the set of all points (x, y) that satisfy the 2 conditions below:

$$-8 \le x \le 5$$
$$-3 \le y \le 4$$

What is the maximum value of $M(x, y)$ when x and y satisfy the 2 conditions given?

    A. 16

    B. 48

    C. 55

    D. 64

    E. 73

13. The function $g(x)$ is graphed in the standard (x, y) coordinate plane below.

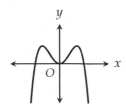

One of the following graphs in the standard (x, y) coordinate plane shows the result of multiplying $g(x)$ by -1. Which graph?

A.

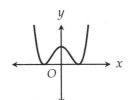

B.

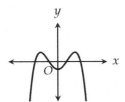

C.

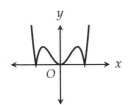

D.

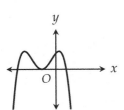

E.

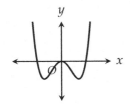

14. Given $f(x) = \dfrac{1 - 2x}{3}$, which of the following expressions is equal to $f^{-1}(x)$ for all real numbers x?

A. $\dfrac{2x - 1}{3}$

B. $\dfrac{3x - 1}{2}$

C. $\dfrac{1 - 3x}{2}$

D. $\dfrac{2}{1 - 3x}$

E. $\dfrac{3}{1 - 2x}$

15. Let $f(x) = ax + 2$ and $g(x) = \sqrt{x + 4}$. In the standard (x, y) coordinate plane, $y = g(f(x))$ passes through $(5, 9)$. What is the value of a?

A. $\dfrac{9}{5}$

B. $\dfrac{7}{3}$

C. 3

D. 5

E. 15

16. Consider the function $g(x) = 2^x$. Which of the following values of x is NOT in the domain of $g^{-1}(x)$?

   I. -1
  II. 0
 III. 1

A. I only

B. II only

C. III only

D. I and II only

E. II and III only

17. The graph of the function $f(x)$ is shown in the standard (x,y) coordinate plane below.

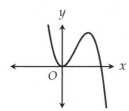

What is the least possible degree of $f(x)$?

A. 0
B. 1
C. 2
D. 3
E. 4

18. The rational function g is defined by $g(x) = \dfrac{x+5}{x^2-9}$. How many asymptotes are there for the graph of $g(x)$?

A. 0 horizontal asymptotes and 2 vertical asymptotes
B. 1 horizontal asymptote and 1 vertical asymptote
C. 1 horizontal asymptote and 2 vertical asymptotes
D. 2 horizontal asymptotes and 0 vertical asymptotes
E. 2 horizontal asymptotes and 1 vertical asymptotes

19. Consider the functions $f(x) = x^2 - 3$ and $g(x) = x + b$, where $b > 0$. One of the following graphs is that of $y = f(g(x))$ in the standard (x,y) coordinate plane. Which one?

A.

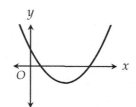

B.

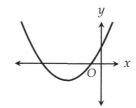

C.

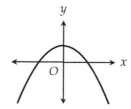

D.

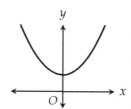

E.

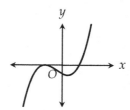

30

20. For a function $f(x)$, $y = 2f(x-1)$ is graphed in the standard (x,y) coordinate plane below.

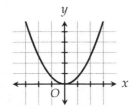

One of the following graphs is the graph of $y = f(x)$. Which one?

A.

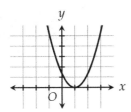

B.

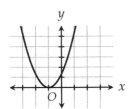

C.

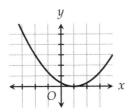

D.

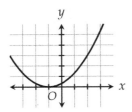

E.

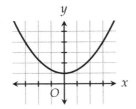

21. The graphs of $f(x)$ and $g(x)$ are shown in the (x,y) coordinate planes below. Which of the following expresses $g(x)$ in terms of $f(x)$?

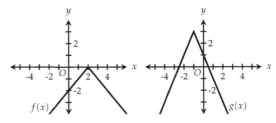

A. $\dfrac{1}{2}f(x-3)+3$

B. $\dfrac{1}{2}f(x+3)-3$

C. $f(x+3)+3$

D. $2f(x-3)+3$

E. $2f(x+3)+3$

22. When $x = t + 3$, the value of the function $f(x)$ is 8 more than the value of $f(x)$ when $x = t + 1$. Which of the following could be the definition of $f(x)$?

A. $x + 10$

B. $2x + 2$

C. $3x + 4$

D. $4x + 6$

E. $6x + 4$

Lines

Answers start on page 105.

1. In the standard (x, y) coordinate plane, what is the x-intercept of the line $y = 3x + 15$?

    A. -5
    B. -3
    C. 3
    D. 5
    E. 15

2. Points $A(4, -2)$ and $B(-5, 4)$ lie in the standard (x, y) coordinate plane. What is the slope of $\overline{AB}$?

    A. $\dfrac{9}{2}$
    B. $\dfrac{2}{3}$
    C. $-\dfrac{2}{9}$
    D. $-\dfrac{1}{2}$
    E. $-\dfrac{2}{3}$

3. When graphed in the standard (x, y) coordinate plane, the line $x + 3y = -6$ crosses the x-axis at which of the following points?

    A. $(-6, 0)$
    B. $(-3, -1)$
    C. $(-2, 0)$
    D. $(0, -2)$
    E. $(6, 0)$

4. In the standard (x, y) coordinate plane, the line $-x + 2y = -6$ is perpendicular to the line:

    A. $y = -2x + 3$
    B. $y = 2x + 3$
    C. $y = -\dfrac{1}{2}x + 3$
    D. $y = \dfrac{1}{2}x - 3$
    E. $y = \dfrac{1}{2}x + 3$

5. One of the following equations is graphed in the standard (x, y) coordinate plane below. Which one?

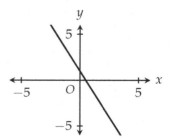

    A. $y = -\dfrac{1}{2}x + 1$
    B. $y = \dfrac{1}{2}x - 1$
    C. $y = -x + 1$
    D. $y = -2x + 1$
    E. $y = 2x + 2$

6. In the standard (x, y) coordinate plane below, the line through the points $(-6, 0)$ and $(4, 0)$ is graphed. Which of the following values is the slope of a line that is in this plane and is parallel to the graphed line?

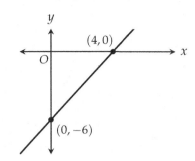

A. $-\dfrac{3}{2}$

B. $-\dfrac{2}{3}$

C. $\dfrac{1}{2}$

D. $\dfrac{2}{3}$

E. $\dfrac{3}{2}$

7. When graphed in the standard (x, y) coordinate plane, the graph of one of the following linear equations is a line perpendicular to the y-axis. Which one?

A. $x = 2$
B. $x = y$
C. $x = 2y$
D. $y = 2$
E. $y = 2x$

8. A line with a slope of 3 passes through the points $(3, k)$ and $(k + 5, 8)$. What is the value of k ?

A. -1
B. $\dfrac{1}{2}$
C. 1
D. $\dfrac{7}{2}$
E. 7

9. When graphed in the standard (x, y) coordinate plane, the line $3x - 4y + 5 = 0$ has a slope of:

A. -3

B. $-\dfrac{3}{4}$

C. $\dfrac{3}{4}$

D. $\dfrac{4}{3}$

E. 3

10. The graph of the equation $3x + 5y = 15$ contains points in which quadrants of the standard (x, y) coordinate plane below?

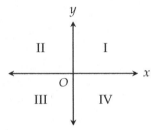

A. II and IV only
B. I, II, and III only
C. I, II, and IV only
D. I, III, and IV only
E. II, III, and IV only

11. What is the area, in square coordinate units, of the region bounded by the lines $y = -\dfrac{1}{2}x + 3$, $x = 0$, and $y = 0$ in the standard (x, y) coordinate plane?

A. 3
B. 6
C. 9
D. 12
E. 18

12. In the standard (x, y) coordinate plane, the region bounded by the x-axis, the y-axis, and the line $y = -\dfrac{1}{2}x + c$ has an area of 36. What is the value of c ?

    A. 3
    B. 6
    C. 8
    D. 9
    E. 12

13. The equations below are linear equations of a system where a and b are nonzero integers.

$$y = \frac{a}{b}x$$
$$y = \frac{b}{a}x$$

    If these equations are graphed in the standard (x, y) coordinate plane, which of the following graphs are possible?

    I.   A single line
    II. Two intersecting lines
    III. Two distinct parallel lines

    A. II only
    B. I and II only
    C. I and III only
    D. II and III only
    E. I, II, and III

13 Quadratics

Answers start on page 107.

1. What is the solution set of $x^2 + 7x - 30 = 0$?

   A. $\{-15, 2\}$
   B. $\{-10, 3\}$
   C. $\{-3, 10\}$
   D. $\{-5, 6\}$
   E. $\{-6, 5\}$

2. One of the following graphs in the standard (x, y) coordinate plane shows a quadratic function with only one real zero. Which one?

   A.

   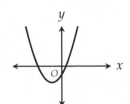

   B.

   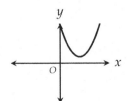

   C.

   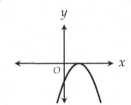

   D.

   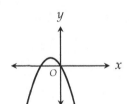

   E.

   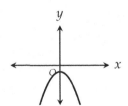

3. Which of the following values of x is in the solution set of the equation $x^2 + 4x - 12 = 9$?

   A. -6
   B. -2
   C. 2
   D. 3
   E. 7

4. The solution set for x of the equation $x^2 + cx - 6 = 0$ is $\{-3, 2\}$. What is the value of c?

   A. -6
   B. -5
   C. -1
   D. 1
   E. 5

5. The equation $x^2 + kx - 12 = 0$ has two solutions. If one of the solutions is $x = -3$, the other solution is:

   A. -4
   B. -2
   C. 2
   D. 4
   E. 6

6. Using the quadratic formula to solve the equation $x^2 + 7x - 5 = 0$ results in which of the following equations?

   A. $x = \dfrac{-7 \pm \sqrt{49 - 4(1)(-5)}}{1}$

   B. $x = \dfrac{-7 \pm \sqrt{49 - 4(1)(-5)}}{2(1)}$

   C. $x = \dfrac{-7 \pm \sqrt{49 + 4(1)(-5)}}{2(1)}$

   D. $x = \dfrac{7 \pm \sqrt{49 - 4(1)(-5)}}{2(1)}$

   E. $x = \dfrac{7 \pm \sqrt{49 - 4(1)(5)}}{2(1)}$

7. Five graphs in the standard (x, y) coordinate plane are shown below. One of the graphs is that of $y = \dfrac{2}{3}(x + 2)^2 - 1$. Which graph is it?

   A.

   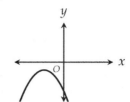

   B.

   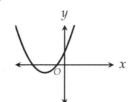

   C.

   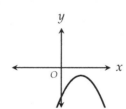

   D.

   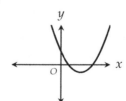

   E.

   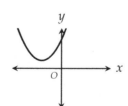

8. Consider the equation $x^2 - kx + 3 = 0$. When solved for x, this equation will have no real solutions for which of the following values of k?

   A. -6
   B. -4
   C. 2
   D. 4
   E. 5

9. In the standard (x, y) coordinate plane, the graph of $y = a(x + 3)^2 - 2$ crosses the x-axis at $(1, 0)$ and at one other point. What is the other point?

   A. $(-7, 0)$
   B. $(-5, 0)$
   C. $(-3, 0)$
   D. $(-1, 0)$
   E. $(5, 0)$

10. The parabola shown in the standard (x, y) plane below is the graph of one of the following equations. Which one?

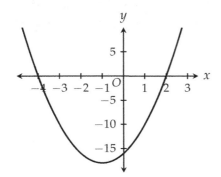

   A. $y = \dfrac{1}{2}(x - 2)(x + 4)$

   B. $y = \dfrac{1}{2}(x + 2)(x - 4)$

   C. $y = (x - 2)(x - 4)$
   D. $y = 2(x - 2)(x + 4)$
   E. $y = 2(x + 2)(x - 4)$

11.
$$h = 3t^2 - 24t - 27$$

   The equation above gives the height above sea level, h km, of a missile t seconds after it is launched. An equivalent factored form of this equation shows that the missile:

   A. is launched from 1 km below sea level.
   B. reaches sea level after 4 seconds.
   C. reaches sea level after 9 seconds.
   D. reaches a maximum height of 1 km.
   E. reaches a maximum height of 9 km.

12. A parabola with vertex (m, n) and axis of symmetry $x = m$ crosses the x-axis at $(m - \sqrt{3}, 0)$. Which of the following points *must* also be on the parabola?

   A. $(-m - \sqrt{3}, 0)$
   B. $(-m + \sqrt{3}, 0)$
   C. $(m + \sqrt{3}, 0)$
   D. $(m^2 + 3, 0)$
   E. Cannot be determined from the given information

14

Coordinate Geometry

Answers start on page 108.

1. A point with coordinates $(8,4)$ in the standard (x,y) coordinate plane is shifted left 5 units and down 9 units. What are the new coordinates of the point?

   A. $(-1,-1)$
   B. $(3,-5)$
   C. $(3,13)$
   D. $(13,-5)$
   E. $(13,13)$

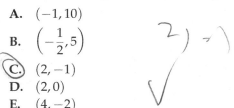

2. In the standard (x,y) coordinate plane, a line segment has endpoints $\left(\frac{3}{2},4\right)$ and $\left(\frac{5}{2},-6\right)$. What is the midpoint of the line segment?

   A. $(-1,10)$
   B. $\left(-\frac{1}{2},5\right)$
   C. $(2,-1)$
   D. $(2,0)$
   E. $(4,-2)$

3. Triangle ABC has vertices in the standard (x,y) coordinate plane at $A(-5,3), B(-1,6)$, and $C(3,5)$. Another triangle $A'B'C'$ has vertices at $A'(-2,1), B'(2,4)$, and $C'(x,y)$. If triangle $A'B'C'$ is a translation of triangle ABC, what are the coordinates of C' ?

   A. $(0,7)$
   B. $(1,8)$
   C. $(5,2)$
   D. $(6,3)$
   E. $(8,5)$

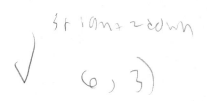

4. A parallelogram is shown in the standard (x, y) coordinate plane below. The coordinates for 3 of its vertices are given. Vertex P is at which of the following points?

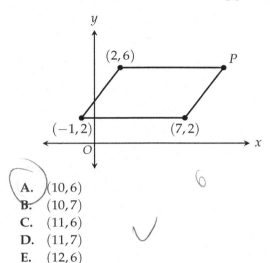

A. $(10, 6)$
B. $(10, 7)$
C. $(11, 6)$
D. $(11, 7)$
E. $(12, 6)$

5. In the standard (x, y) coordinate plane, the point $(3, -8)$ is the midpoint of a line segment with endpoints $(1, -12)$ and (a, b). What is the value of $a + b$?

A. -16
B. -8
C. 1
D. 6
E. 12

6. In the standard (x, y) coordinate plane, a curve that is symmetric with respect to the x-axis crosses the point (p, q). The curve must also cross which of the following points?

A. $(q, -p)$
B. (q, p)
C. $(-p, -q)$
D. $(-p, q)$
E. $(p, -q)$

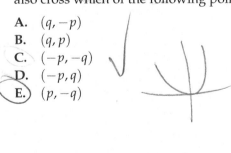

Use the following information to answer questions 7–8.

Triangle ABC is shown below in the standard (x, y) coordinate plane.

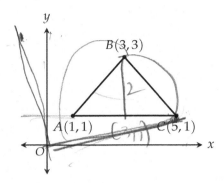

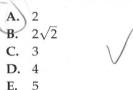

7. What is the length, in coordinate units, of the altitude from B to $\overline{AC}$?

A. 2
B. $2\sqrt{2}$
C. 3
D. 4
E. 5

8. Which of the following are the new coordinates of C after a $90°$ counterclockwise rotation about the origin?

A. $(-5, -1)$
B. $(-5, 1)$
C. $(-1, -5)$
D. $(-1, 5)$
E. $(1, 5)$

9. When the locations of two airports are plotted in the standard (x, y) coordinate plane, the first airport has coordinates $(6, 4)$ and the second airport has coordinates $(-3, 12)$. If 1 coordinate unit represents 20 miles, which of the following best approximates the straight-line distance, in miles, between these two airports?

A. 200
B. 240
C. 280
D. 320
E. 360

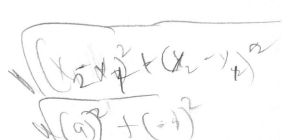

10. Triangle ABC has vertices $A(2,-3)$, $B(2,5)$, and $C(6,-3)$ in the standard (x,y) coordinate plane shown below. A circle (not shown) circumscribes triangle ABC. Which of the following are the coordinates of the center of the circle?

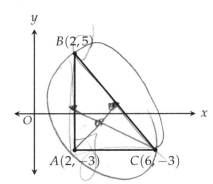

A. $(2,0.5)$
B. $(2,1)$
C. $(4,-3)$
D. $(4,1)$
E. $(5,-1)$

11. Point $M(-3,2)$ is shown in the standard (x,y) coordinate plane below. Point M is reflected across the line $y=8$ to point M' (not shown). What are the coordinates of M' ?

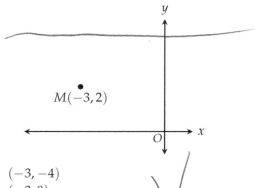

A. $(-3,-4)$
B. $(-3,8)$
C. $(-3,10)$
D. $(-3,14)$
E. $(2,2)$

12. Trapezoid $ABCD$ is graphed in the standard (x,y) coordinate plane below. What is the distance, in coordinate units, from the midpoint of $\overline{AB}$ to the midpoint of $\overline{CD}$?

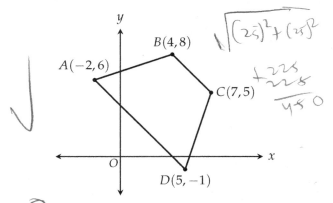

A. $\sqrt{50}$
B. $\sqrt{68}$
C. $\sqrt{72}$
D. $\sqrt{130}$
E. $\sqrt{200}$

13. In the standard (x,y) coordinate plane below, point A has coordinates $(2,7)$ and point A' is the projection of A onto the line $y=x$. What are the coordinates of A' ?

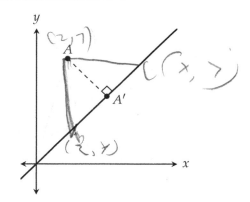

A. $(3,3)$
B. $(4,4)$
C. $(4.25,4.25)$
D. $(4.5,4.5)$
E. $(5,5)$

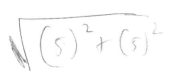

15
Angles

Answers start on page 111.

1. In the figure below, D is on $\overleftrightarrow{CE}$, the measure of $\angle DAC$ equals $24°$, the measure of $\angle DCA$ equals $80°$, and the measure of $\angle BDE$ equals $40°$. What is the measure of $\angle ADB$?

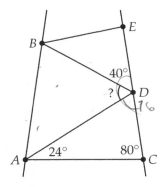

   A. $54°$
   B. $58°$
   C. $64°$
   D. $69°$
   E. $71°$

2. In the figure below, line m is parallel to line n. Points A and B are on line m, and points C and D are on line n. What is the value of y ?

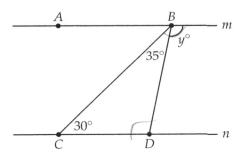

   A. 105
   B. 115
   C. 125
   D. 135
   E. 145

41

3. In the plane shown in the figure below, lines m and n are cut by transversal l. Lines m and n are parallel. Which of the following statements *must* be true?

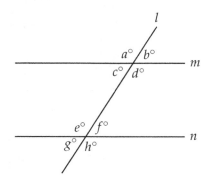

A. $a + e = 90$
B. $c + e = 90$
C. $a + d = 180$
D. $b + c = 180$
E. $d + g = 180$

4. In parallelogram $ABCD$ below, the measure of $\angle BAC$ is 86° and the measure of $\angle BCA$ is 34°. What is the measure of $\angle BCD$?

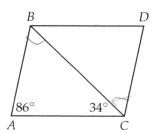

A. 34°
B. 48°
C. 52°
D. 60°
E. 65°

5. Triangle $\triangle ABC$ and collinear points C, B, and D are shown in the figure below. The measure of $\angle A$ is $a°$, the measure of $\angle ABC$ is $b°$, the measure of $\angle C$ is 67°, and the measure of $\angle ABD$ is $(a + b)°$. What is the value of a ?

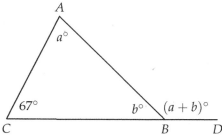

A. 21°
B. 38°
C. 46°
D. 52°
E. 67°

$113 = a + b$
$2b + a = 40$

6. In the figure below, $\overline{AB}$ is perpendicular to $\overline{AC}$ and $\overline{AD}$ is perpendicular to $\overline{BC}$.

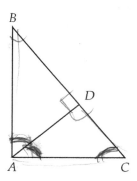

Which of the following pairs of angles do NOT necessarily sum to 90° ?

A. $\angle ABD$ and $\angle ACD$
B. $\angle ABD$ and $\angle BAD$
C. $\angle ACD$ and $\angle CAD$
D. $\angle BAD$ and $\angle CAD$
E. $\angle BAD$ and $\angle ACD$

7. In the diagram below, two rays of light enter a thick pane of glass. The angle at which a ray of light strikes a pane of glass is equal in measure to the angle at which it is reflected. What is the measure of the indicated angle?

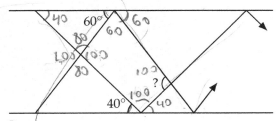

   A. 100°
   B. 105°
   C. 110°
   D. 120°
   E. 125°

8. In the figure below, $\overline{BC}$ is parallel to $\overline{DE}$, the measure of $\angle B$ is 38°, and the measure of $\angle D$ is 87°. What is the measure of $\angle BAF$?

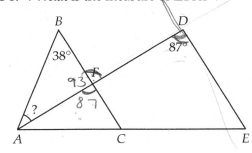

   A. 42°
   B. 46°
   C. 49°
   D. 52°
   E. 55°

9. In the figure below, $\overline{AD}$ and $\overline{BC}$ intersect at E. What is the value of y?

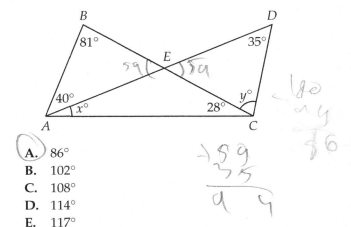

   A. 86°
   B. 102°
   C. 108°
   D. 114°
   E. 117°

10. In the figure below, $\overline{AB}$ is parallel to $\overline{ED}$, the measure of $\angle CDE$ is 33°, and the measure of $\angle ACD$ is 118°. What is the measure of $\angle CAB$?

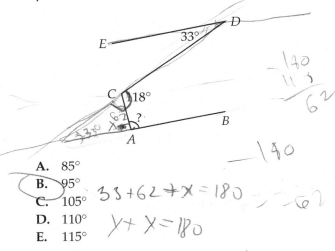

   A. 85°
   B. 95°
   C. 105°
   D. 110°
   E. 115°

11. A regular octagon is shown below. If it can be determined, what is the value of $x + y$?

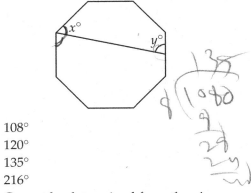

   A. 108°
   B. 120°
   C. 135°
   D. 216°
   E. Cannot be determined from the given information

43

16

Triangles

Answers start on page 113.

1. In $\triangle ABC$ below, $\angle A$ is a right angle and the measure of $\angle B$ is $45°$. What is the length, in meters, of $\overline{BC}$?

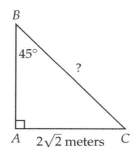

A. 2
B. $2\sqrt{6}$
C. 4
D. $4\sqrt{2}$
E. 8

2. For $\triangle XYZ$ shown below, which of the following is an expression for h in terms of k ?

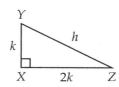

A. $\sqrt{5k}$
B. $k\sqrt{5}$
C. $5k$
D. $5k^2$
E. $25k^2$

3. The 2 legs of a right triangle have lengths 6 inches and 10 inches. The length of the hypotenuse, in inches, is between:

A. 7 and 9
B. 9 and 10
C. 10 and 11
D. 11 and 12
E. 12 and 14

4. In the figure shown below, $\overline{AB} \parallel \overline{CD}$, $\overline{AD}$ and $\overline{BC}$ intersect at E, and the given lengths are in feet. What is the length, in feet, of $\overline{AB}$?

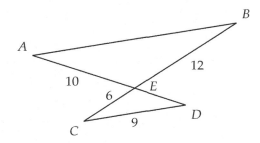

A. 16
B. 18
C. 19
D. 20
E. 21

5. For all triangles $\triangle KLM$ where the measure of $\angle L$ is greater than the measure of $\angle M$, such as the triangle shown below, which of the following mathematical statements involving the lengths of the sides of $\triangle KLM$ is true?

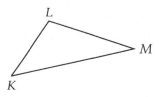

A. $KL = KM$
B. $KL > KM$
C. $KL \geq KM$
D. $KL < KM$
E. $KL \leq KM$

6. Which of the following sets of 3 numbers could be the side lengths, in inches, of a right triangle?

A. 2, 2, 2
B. 4, 5, 6
C. 5, 7, 9
D. 8, 10, 16
E. 9, 12, 15

7. In $\triangle ABC$ below, $\overline{BC}$ is $6\sqrt{3}$ feet long, the measure of $\angle C$ is $30°$, and $\angle B$ is a right angle. What is the length, in feet, of $\overline{AC}$?

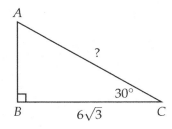

A. $3\sqrt{3}$
B. 9
C. 12
D. $12\sqrt{3}$
E. 18

8. In the figure below, $\triangle ABC$ and $\triangle DEF$ are similar triangles such that $\angle A \cong \angle D$ and $\angle B \cong \angle F$. The given lengths are in centimeters. What is the length, in centimeters, of $\overline{DE}$?

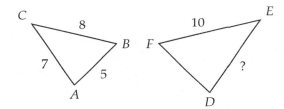

A. $6\frac{1}{4}$
B. 7
C. $8\frac{3}{4}$
D. 9
E. $9\frac{3}{4}$

9. A manufacturing plant is located 12 miles south and 9 miles east of Central Station. To fulfill orders, the plant sends its goods to the shipping center, which is located 18 miles north and 7 miles west of Central Station. What is the distance, in miles, between the plant and the shipping center?

A. 32
B. 34
C. 36
D. 42
E. 48

10. Shown below are right triangles $\triangle ABC$ and $\triangle DEC$ with lengths given in feet. What is the length, in feet, of $\overline{CD}$?

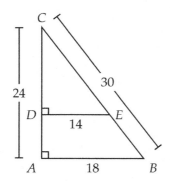

A. $9\dfrac{1}{3}$

B. $15\dfrac{3}{5}$

C. $16\dfrac{1}{3}$

D. $16\dfrac{3}{4}$

E. $18\dfrac{2}{3}$

11. Which of the following sets of 3 numbers could be the side lengths, in meters, of an acute triangle? (Note: An acute triangle has 3 angles whose measures are each less than 90°.)

A. $\{5, 5, 8\}$
B. $\{5, 12, 13\}$
C. $\{6, 9, 12\}$
D. $\{7, 8, 10\}$
E. $\{9, 12, 15\}$

12. The sides of a right triangle are 9 inches, 12 inches, and 15 inches long. A second right triangle similar to the first has a hypotenuse that is 9 inches long. To the nearest tenth of an inch, what is the length of the shortest side of the second triangle?

A. 3.0
B. 5.4
C. 6.0
D. 6.8
E. 7.2

13. In $\triangle ABC$ below, $\angle B$ is a right angle and the given side lengths are in meters. What is the value of k ?

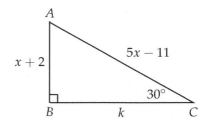

A. 3
B. 6
C. $5\sqrt{3}$
D. $7\sqrt{3}$
E. 9

14. For the triangles in the figure below, the ratio of the perimeter of $\triangle ABC$ to the perimeter of $\triangle ABD$ is equivalent to which of the following ratios of side lengths?

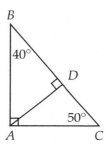

A. $AB:AD$
B. $AB:BD$
C. $AC:AB$
D. $AC:BD$
E. $BC:AD$

15. Let $\triangle ABC$ and $\triangle DEF$ be isosceles right triangles such that the legs of $\triangle ABC$ are 2 feet longer than the legs of $\triangle DEF$. By how many feet is the hypotenuse of $\triangle ABC$ longer than the hypotenuse of $\triangle DEF$?

A. $\sqrt{2}$
B. 2
C. $2\sqrt{2}$
D. 4
E. $4\sqrt{2}$

16. The height of rhombus $WXYZ$ shown below is 3 meters and the measure of $\angle W$ is 60°. What is the area, in square meters, of $WXYZ$? (Note: A rhombus is a parallelogram with 4 congruent sides.)

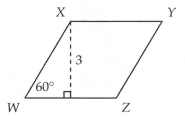

A. $6\sqrt{2}$
B. $6\sqrt{3}$
C. 9
D. $9\sqrt{3}$
E. 12

17. The figure below shows a pyramid with equilateral triangular faces and a square base of side length 8 inches. What is the height, in inches, of the pyramid?

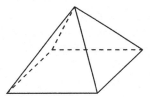

A. $3\sqrt{3}$
B. $3\sqrt{6}$
C. $4\sqrt{2}$
D. $4\sqrt{3}$
E. $4\sqrt{6}$

17
Circles

Answers start on page 116.

1. In the standard (x, y) coordinate plane, what are the coordinates of the center of the circle with equation $(x + \sqrt{3})^2 + (y - 2\sqrt{2})^2 = 4$?

    A. $(-2\sqrt{2}, \sqrt{3})$
    B. $(2\sqrt{2}, -\sqrt{3})$
    C. $(-\sqrt{3}, -2\sqrt{2})$
    D. $(-\sqrt{3}, 2\sqrt{2})$
    E. $(\sqrt{3}, -2\sqrt{2})$

2. Circle A has a diameter of $2x$ inches and Circle B has a diameter of $6x$ inches. What is the ratio of the area of Circle A to the area of Circle B ?

    A. 1:3
    B. 1:6
    C. 1:9
    D. 1:12
    E. 2:3

3. A circle in the standard (x, y) coordinate plane has center $(-3, 1)$ and diameter 10 coordinate units. Which of the following is an equation of the circle?

    A. $(x + 3)^2 + (y - 1)^2 = 100$
    B. $(x - 3)^2 + (y + 1)^2 = 10$
    C. $(x - 3)^2 + (y + 1)^2 = 25$
    D. $(x + 3)^2 + (y - 1)^2 = 10$
    E. $(x + 3)^2 + (y - 1)^2 = 25$

4. Four points, $A, B, C,$ and D lie on a circle having a circumference of 16 units. B is 5 units clockwise from A. C is 12 units counterclockwise from B. D is 14 units counterclockwise from A. What is the order of the points, starting with A and going clockwise around the circle?

    A. A, B, D, C
    B. A, B, C, D
    C. A, C, D, B
    D. A, D, C, B
    E. A, D, B, C

5. What is the length, in inches, of a 75° arc of a circle whose area is 144π square inches?

    A. $\dfrac{5}{2}$
    B. $\dfrac{5\pi}{2}$
    C. 5
    D. 5π
    E. 10

48

6. Points A through F lie on the circle shown below so that the distance between any 2 adjacent points is equal. Chord $\overline{EF}$ is 4 inches long. What is the length, in inches, of the diameter of the circle?

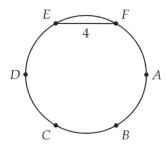

A. 5
B. $4\sqrt{3}$
C. $6\sqrt{4}$
D. 8
E. 10

7. As shown in the figure below, A is the center of the circle, $\overline{BC}$ is tangent to the circle at C, and $\overline{AC}$ has a length of 6 cm. The shaded region inside the circle and outside the triangle has an area of 31π square centimeters. What is the measure of $\angle ABC$?

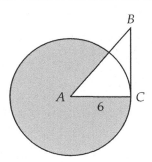

A. 40°
B. 45°
C. 50°
D. 55°
E. 60°

8. The shaded sector of the circle shown below is bounded by radius $\overline{AB}$, radius $\overline{AC}$, and minor arc $\overset{\frown}{BC}$. The length of $\overline{AB}$ is 5 cm, and the area of the shaded sector is 10π square centimeters. What is the measure of $\angle BAC$?

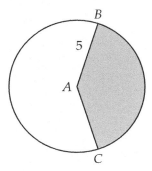

A. 135°
B. 140°
C. 144°
D. 150°
E. 156°

9. A dartboard consists of 3 concentric circles, as shown below. The radius of the outer circle is 14 inches, and the distance between adjacent circles is 5 inches. What is the area, in square inches, of the inner circle of the dartboard?

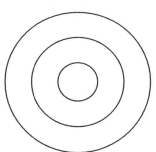

A. 4π
B. 8π
C. 10π
D. 16π
E. 25π

10. Three congruent circles, each with a radius of 2 inches, are shown in the figure below. Each circle is tangent to the other two circles. What is the perimeter, in inches, of the shaded region?

A. π

B. 2π

C. $\dfrac{5\pi}{2}$

D. 3π

E. $\dfrac{7\pi}{2}$

11. In the circle shown below, radius $\overline{OB}$ is 12 inches long, chord $\overline{AC}$ is 16 inches long, and $\overline{OB}$ is perpendicular to $\overline{AC}$ at D. How many inches long is $\overline{OD}$?

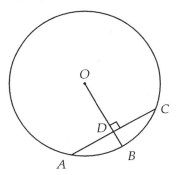

A. $4\sqrt{2}$

B. $4\sqrt{5}$

C. $5\sqrt{2}$

D. $5\sqrt{5}$

E. 10

12. In the figure below, $\overline{AB}$ is tangent to two circles with centers 12 inches apart. The larger circle has a radius of 5 inches, and the smaller circle has a radius of 1 inch. What is the length, in inches, of $\overline{AB}$?

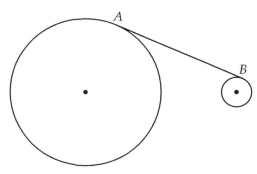

A. $4\sqrt{10}$

B. $6\sqrt{2}$

C. $8\sqrt{2}$

D. 10

E. 13

13. In the standard (x, y) coordinate plane, what is the area, in square coordinate units, of the circle whose equation is $x^2 - 10x + y^2 + 6y - 15 = 0$?

A. 25π

B. 36π

C. 49π

D. 64π

E. 81π

18

Area & Perimeter

Answers start on page 119.

1. A rectangle has a perimeter of 28 meters and a width of 6 meters. What is the area, in square meters, of the rectangle?

   A. 48
   B. 56
   C. 60
   D. 66
   E. 96

2. In the figure below, each of the 7 small squares has an area of 9 square feet. What is the area of the shaded region, in square feet?

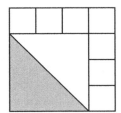

   A. 18
   B. 36.5
   C. 40.5
   D. 54.5
   E. 60

3. A hexagon has 1 side of length x cm, 2 sides of length $(x - 1)$ cm each, and 3 sides of length $(2x + 1)$ cm each. What is the perimeter, in centimeters, of the hexagon?

   A. $8x + 1$
   B. $8x + 2$
   C. $9x$
   D. $9x - 1$
   E. $9x + 1$

4. A triangle with a base of 16 inches and a height of 10 inches has an area that is 5 times the area of a rectangle with a width of 8 inches. What is the height, in inches, of the rectangle?

   A. 2
   B. 4
   C. 8
   D. 16
   E. 32

5. If the area of rectangle *ABEF* in the figure below is 48 square inches, what is the area of trapezoid *ACDF*, in square inches?

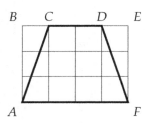

   A. 18
   B. 24
   C. 30
   D. 36
   E. 40

6. A walkway is constructed from 6 congruent square tiles, as shown below. The total area of the walkway is 54 square feet. What is the perimeter, in feet, of the walkway?

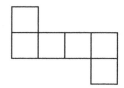

   A. 42
   B. 45
   C. 48
   D. 51
   E. 54

7. Twenty-five cubes are placed side by side in a line as shown below. The edges of each cube are 1 centimeter long. What is the surface area, in square centimeters, of the resulting figure?

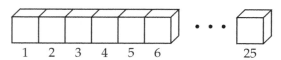

   A. 25
   B. 27
   C. 100
   D. 102
   E. 104

8. In the figure below, two congruent isosceles triangles *ABC* and *DEF* intersect so that *B* and *E* are the midpoints of $\overline{DF}$ and $\overline{AC}$ respectively. If the area of the shaded region is 10 square units, what is the area of triangle *ABC*, in square units?

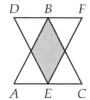

   A. 12
   B. 15
   C. 18
   D. 20
   E. 25

9. In the figure below, a square with a side length of 10 inches is formed by 4 congruent rectangles and an inner square with a side length of 6 inches. What is the area, in square inches, of the shaded rectangle?

   A. 12
   B. 16
   C. 18
   D. 20
   E. 24

10. The base of a triangle is increased by 30% and the height is increased by 20%. By what percentage does the area of the triangle increase?

   A. 35%
   B. 40%
   C. 50%
   D. 56%
   E. 58%

11. Jody folds a rectangular piece of paper to form the trapezoid shown below; the given dimensions are in inches. Which of the following is closest to the perimeter, in inches, of the trapezoid?

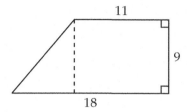

A. 40
B. 45
C. 50
D. 55
E. 60

12. In the figure below, all line segments are measured in feet and have integer lengths. The areas of three rectangles are given in square feet. What is the area of rectangle $WXYZ$, in square feet?

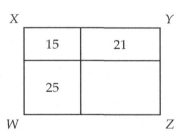

A. 90
B. 96
C. 98
D. 102
E. 108

13. Two rectangles intersect in right angles as shown below. The given lengths are in feet. What is the area, in square feet, of the shaded region?

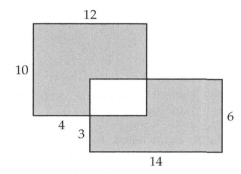

A. 132
B. 156
C. 174
D. 180
E. 204

14. A cardboard box with a cover is opened and flattened to form the figure shown below. The given lengths are in inches. What is the total area, in square inches, of the figure?

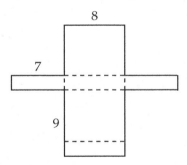

A. 150
B. 156
C. 172
D. 180
E. 192

15. Robert designs a company logo in the shape of a parallelogram. The perimeter of the logo is 60 cm, and the length of 1 side is 12 cm. If it can be determined, what are the lengths, in cm, of the other 3 sides of the logo?

   A. 12, 12, 36
   B. 12, 15, 15
   C. 12, 16, 20
   D. 12, 18, 18
   E. Cannot be determine from the given information

16. In the figure below, the outer square contains squares X, Y, and Z. Their areas are 16, 25, and 16 square centimeters, respectively. What is the area of the shaded region, in square centimeters?

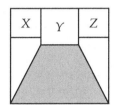

   A. 32
   B. 40
   C. 64
   D. 72
   E. 81

17. The sides of a square are split into thirds by the sides of an octagon, as shown below. The side length of the square is 12 feet. What is the area, in square feet, of the shaded region?

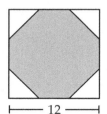

   A. 104
   B. 112
   C. 120
   D. 128
   E. 136

18. For trapezoid $WXYZ$ shown below, $WX = 7$ ft, $YZ = 6$ ft, and the perimeter is 32 ft. What is the area, in square feet, of $WXYZ$?

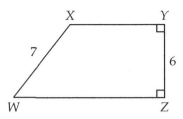

   A. 49
   B. 57
   C. 65
   D. 96
   E. 114

19. The ratio of the side lengths of a rectangle with an area of 200 square inches is 5 : 1. Which of the following is closest to the length, in inches, of the *shorter* side of the rectangle?

   A. 5
   B. 6
   C. 7
   D. 8
   E. 9

20. The owner of a tennis court paints a 4-foot-wide border along all 4 sides of the court, as shown below. The outer edge of the painted border is 44 feet long and 86 feet wide.

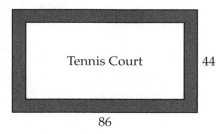

The owner plans to add an extra layer of cement to the tennis court, using cement that has a price of $9 per bag. The owner can buy only full bags of cement and each bag will cover an area of 75 square feet of the tennis court. What is the total price of the cement that the owner needs to buy?

A. $324
B. $333
C. $342
D. $351
E. $360

21. The vertices of a trapezoid have the (x, y) coordinates indicated in the figure below. What is the area, in square coordinate units, of the trapezoid?

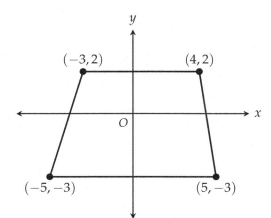

A. 28.5
B. 32
C. 37.5
D. 42.5
E. 50

22. The floor of a room that is 22 feet long and 30 feet wide is covered with 2-ft-by-2-ft tiles, some black and some green. The green tiles are used only for the border of the room. The rest are black. How many green tiles are there?

A. 26
B. 32
C. 48
D. 50
E. 52

23. For $\triangle ABC$ shown below, $\overline{AB}$ has a length of 6 inches and $\overline{BC}$ has a length of 8 inches. If $\angle ABC$ and $\angle ADB$ are right angles, what is the length, in inches, of $\overline{AD}$?

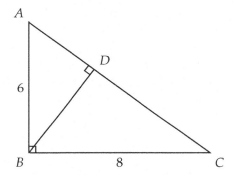

A. 3.6
B. 4.8
C. 6.4
D. 7.2
E. 9

24. In the figure shown below, $\overline{AB}$ is a diameter of the smaller semicircle and a radius of the larger semicircle. What is the ratio of the area of the shaded region to the area of the unshaded region?

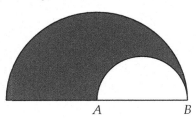

A. 2 : 1
B. 3 : 1
C. 3 : 2
D. 4 : 3
E. 5 : 3

19 Volume

Answers start on page 124.

1. The diameter and height of the right circular cylinder shown below are given in inches. What is the volume, in cubic inches, of the cylinder?

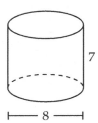

   A. 56π
   B. 88π
   C. 112π
   D. 392π
   E. 448π

2. The volume, V, of a rectangular prism is given by $V = lwh$, where l is the length of the base, w is the width of the base, and h is the height of the prism. A rectangular prism has a square base, a height of 8 inches, and a volume of 216 cubic inches. What is the width, in inches, of the base of the prism?

   A. $3\sqrt{3}$
   B. 6
   C. 9
   D. 27
   E. 36

3. The hemisphere shown below has a radius of 4 feet. Which of the following is closest to the volume, in cubic feet, of the hemisphere? (Note: The volume of a sphere is given by $\frac{4}{3}\pi r^3$, where r is the radius.)

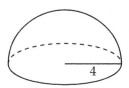

   A. 134
   B. 151
   C. 201
   D. 268
   E. 536

4. What is the volume, in cubic inches, of a cube that has a surface area of 384 square inches?

   A. 64
   B. 512
   C. 4,096
   D. 32,768
   E. 262,144

5. A right circular cylinder has a radius of x inches and a height of 2 inches. If the volume of the cylinder is 16 cubic inches, what is the value of x ?

   (Note: The volume of a cylinder with radius r and height h is $\pi r^2 h$.)

   A. $\sqrt{\dfrac{8}{\pi}}$

   B. $\sqrt{\dfrac{32}{\pi}}$

   C. $\dfrac{2}{\sqrt{\pi}}$

   D. $\dfrac{4}{\pi}$

   E. $\sqrt{8\pi}$

6. A right circular cone shown below has a base diameter of 8 inches and a volume of 250 cubic inches. Which of the following is closest to the height, in inches, of the cone?

   (Note: The volume of a cone with radius r and height h is $\dfrac{1}{3}\pi r^2 h$.)

   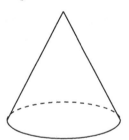

   A. 12
   B. 15
   C. 18
   D. 21
   E. 24

7. Each edge of a cube is $(x - 2)$ centimeters long. The volume of the cube is 10 cubic centimeters. What is the value of x ?

   A. $\sqrt[3]{12}$
   B. $\sqrt[3]{2} + \sqrt[3]{10}$
   C. $2 + \sqrt[3]{10}$
   D. $2 + \sqrt{10}$
   E. $5\sqrt{2}$

8. The container shown below is in the shape of a right rectangular prism with dimensions given in meters. The container is full of water and needs to be drained to 40% of its capacity. How many cubic meters of water should be drained from the container?

   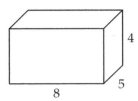

   A. 64
   B. 72
   C. 80
   D. 88
   E. 96

9. A formula used to calculate the volume, V, of a right circular cylinder is $V = \pi r^2 h$, where r is the radius and h is the height. For a construction project, an engineer uses two right circular cylinders made out of plastic. The first has radius R inches and height H inches, and the second has radius $2R$ inches and height $\dfrac{1}{2}H$ inches. In terms of R and H, the volume of the second cylinder is how many cubic inches greater than the volume of the first cylinder?

   A. 0
   B. $\pi R^2 H$
   C. $2\pi R^2 H$
   D. $3\pi R^2 H$
   E. $4\pi R^2 H$

10. Boxes A and B are both rectangular prisms. The area of the base of Box A is 3 times the area of the base of Box B. The height of Box A is 2 times the height of Box B. The volume of Box A is how many times the volume of Box B?

   A. 5
   B. 6
   C. 8
   D. 12
   E. 18

20

Systems of Equations

Answers start on page 126.

1. Given that $2x + 5y = 27$ and $-3x + 4y = -6$, what is the value of xy ?

   A. 12
   B. 15
   C. 18
   D. 21
   E. 24

2. In the (x, y) solution to the system of equations below, $y = $?

   $$\frac{1}{2}x = \frac{3}{4}y$$
   $$2x + 5y = -16$$

   A. -3
   B. -2
   C. 2
   D. 4
   E. 6

3. Which of the following (a, b) pairs is the solution for the system of equations $2a - b = 6$ and $-a + 2b = 9$?

   A. $(-8, -22)$
   B. $(-7, -20)$
   C. $(5, 4)$
   D. $(7, 8)$
   E. $(8, 10)$

4. For what value of c would the following system of equations have an infinite number of solutions?

   $$3x + 7y = 12$$
   $$x + cy = 4$$

   A. -1
   B. $\dfrac{3}{7}$
   C. $\dfrac{7}{3}$
   D. 5
   E. 21

5. On a trivia show, Seth receives 3 points for each correct answer but loses 2 points for each incorrect answer. He answered a total of 20 questions and ended up with 40 points. Which of the following systems of equations, when solved, gives the number of questions he answered correctly, x, and the number of questions he answered incorrectly, y, on the show?

A. $x + y = 40$
    $3x + 2y = 20$

B. $x + y = 40$
    $3x - 2y = 20$

C. $x + y = 20$
    $3x + 2y = 40$

D. $x + y = 20$
    $3x - 2y = 40$

E. $x + y = 20$
    $2x - 3y = 40$

6. At a carnival, a food stall sold bags of cotton candy for $5 each and bags of popcorn for $7 each. A total of 140 bags were sold for $820. How many bags of cotton candy did the stall sell?

A. 40
B. 50
C. 60
D. 70
E. 80

7. For which of the following values of a and b would the following system of equations have infinitely many solutions?

$$ax - 3y = 6$$
$$8x - 6y = b$$

A. $a = 4, b = 3$
B. $a = 4, b = 12$
C. $a = 8, b = 6$
D. $a = 16, b = 3$
E. $a = 16, b = 12$

8. The table below gives the number of seconds it takes to print 1 page at Pete's Copy Center for different printer and color combinations.

Type of Printer	Black & White	Color
Inkjet	2	3
Laser	1.5	2

Mackey brought a 50-page manuscript to Pete's Copy Center and printed it in 84 seconds using a laser printer. Some of the pages were printed in black and white and some were printed in color. How many pages did Mackey print in black and white?

A. 14
B. 18
C. 24
D. 32
E. 36

9. The system of equations below has multiple solutions (x, y) such that $y = \dfrac{5}{3}x - 2$. What is the value of k?

$$10x - 6y = k$$
$$-5x + 3y = -6$$

A. -12
B. -3
C. 2
D. 6
E. 12

10. A playlist contains 25 songs and runs for a total of 80 minutes. It consists of x 2-minute songs and y 3-minute songs. Which of the following systems of equations, when solved, gives the number of 2-minute songs and 3-minute songs in the playlist?

   A. $x + y = 25$
         $6xy = 80$

   B. $x + y = 25$
         $2x + 3y = 80$

   C. $x + y = 80$
         $2x + 3y = 25$

   D. $x + y = 25$
         $3x + 2y = 80$

   E. $x + y = 80$
         $3x + 2y = 25$

11. To mail out invitations to a conference, Mr. Miller bought 65 envelopes for $11. A small envelope costs $0.10 and a large envelope costs $0.25. How many large envelopes did he buy?

   A.   25
   B.   30
   C.   35
   D.   40
   E.   45

12. Which of the following is equal to the value of x in the solution of the system of equations below?

$$ax + y = 2$$
$$bx + 2y = 1$$

   A. $\dfrac{5}{2a + b}$

   B. $\dfrac{3}{2a - b}$

   C. $\dfrac{3}{a + 2b}$

   D. $\dfrac{1}{2a - b}$

   E. $\dfrac{1}{a - 2b}$

21

Inequalities

Answers start on page 129.

1. Which of the following inequalities is equivalent to $4x - 6y < 7x - 9$?

   A. $x > -2y - 3$
   B. $x > -2y + 3$
   C. $x < -2y + 3$
   D. $x > 2y - 3$
   E. $x < 2y - 3$

2. To ensure there is enough room for all the food at a student banquet, Alice decides to buy whole pizzas such that there are no more than 200 slices. The whole pizzas made by the local pizzeria come in two sizes: medium and large. A medium pizza contains 6 slices and a large pizza contains 8 slices. In the following inequalities, x represents the number of medium pizzas and y represents the number of large pizzas. Which inequality expresses the constraint on the number of pizzas Alice will buy?

   A. $6x + 8y \leq 200$
   B. $6x + 8y \geq 200$
   C. $8x + 6y \leq 200$
   D. $8x + 6y \geq 200$
   E. $\dfrac{x}{6} + \dfrac{y}{8} \leq 200$

3. The statement below can be expressed algebraically as which of the following inequalities?

   5 more than the product of 8 and a number b is less than 3 times the square of a number a

   A. $5 - 8b < 6a$
   B. $5 - 8b < 3a^2$
   C. $5 + 8b < 6a$
   D. $5 + 8b < 3 + a^2$
   E. $5 + 8b < 3a^2$

4. Which of the following graphs shows the solution set for x of $-4x - 7 \leq 5$?

   A.

   B.

   C.
   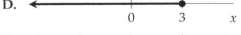

   D.

   E.

5. Susie had 60 tickets to use for the games at the arcade. She spent 6 tickets on Game A and 12 tickets on Game B. Susie still wants to play c rounds of Game C and d rounds of Game D. Each round of Game C requires 3 tickets and each round of Game D requires 5 tickets. Which of the following inequalities represents the number of rounds of Game C and Game D Susie can play with her remaining tickets?

   A. $3c + 5d \leq 60$
   B. $5c + 3d \leq 60$
   C. $3c + 5d < 42$
   D. $3c + 5d \leq 42$
   E. $5c + 3d \leq 42$

6. What is the smallest integer y that satisfies the inequality $\frac{1}{5}y - \frac{1}{2}y < -2$?

   A. 5
   B. 6
   C. 7
   D. 8
   E. 10

7. Which of the following is equivalent to $\dfrac{2x - 7}{3} - 1 < 0$?

   A. $x < -2$
   B. $x < 0$
   C. $x < 5$
   D. $x < 8$
   E. $x < 10$

8. For real numbers a and b such that $a^2 > b^2$, which of the following *must* be true?

   A. $a > b$
   B. $b > a$
   C. $a + b > 0$
   D. $|a| > |b|$
   E. $-a^2 > -b^2$

9. If x and y are real numbers such that $x \geq 2$ and $y \leq -2$, then which of the following statements about xy *must* be true?

   A. $xy \leq -4$
   B. $xy \geq -4$
   C. $xy \leq 0$
   D. $xy \geq 0$
   E. $-2 \leq xy \leq 2$

10. The solution set of $|x - b| \leq 4$, where b is a real number, is $\{x \mid 3 \leq x \leq 11\}$. What is the value of b ?

   A. -7
   B. -1
   C. 1
   D. 7
   E. 15

11. The values of real numbers x, y, and z are constrained by the 2 conditions below.

   1. x is 3 more than y
   2. y is more than z subtracted by 5

Which of the following inequalities expresses the relationship between x and z according to the 2 conditions?

   A. $x > z - 2$
   B. $x < z - 2$
   C. $x > z - 8$
   D. $x < z - 8$
   E. $x > z + 2$

12. Which of the following inequalities is equivalent to $\sqrt{|x| + 1} \leq 3$?

   A. $-1 \leq x \leq 8$
   B. $-2 \leq x \leq 2$
   C. $-4 \leq x \leq 4$
   D. $-8 \leq x \leq 8$
   E. $-10 \leq x \leq 8$

13. Which of the following graphs in the standard (x, y) coordinate plane best represents the solution set to the system of inequalities below?

$$0 \leq x \leq 5$$
$$5 \leq y \leq 10$$
$$y \geq x + 2$$

A.

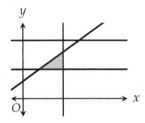

B.

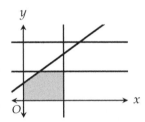

C.

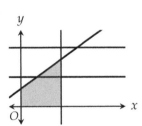

D.

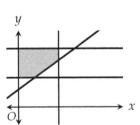

E.

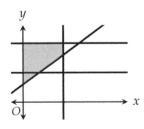

14. Which of the following is the graph of the solution set of $|x - 2a| \geq 6$?

15. Given that constants a and b are positive real numbers, which of the following graphs in the standard (x, y) coordinate plane is that of $y < ax + b$?

A.

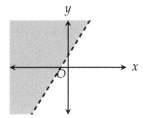

B.

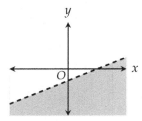

C.

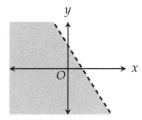

D.

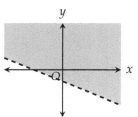

E.

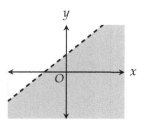

22 Trigonometry

Answers start on page 132.

1. The lengths of two sides of right triangle △DEF shown below are given in feet. What is the value of tan F ?

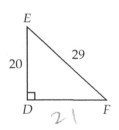

21

A. $\frac{20}{21}$

B. $\frac{20}{23}$

C. $\frac{20}{29}$

D. $\frac{21}{20}$

E. $\frac{21}{29}$

2. In right triangle △XYZ shown below, the given dimensions are in centimeters. Which of the following trigonometric expressions is equal to $\frac{15}{17}$?

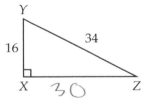

30

A. cos Y
B. tan Y
C. sin Z
D. cos Z
E. tan Z

3. At a point on level ground 80 meters from the base of a tree, the angle of elevation to the top of the tree is 55°. Which of the following best approximates the height of the tree, in meters?
(Note: sin 55° ≈ 0.82, cos 55° ≈ 0.57, tan 55° ≈ 1.43)

A. 46
B. 56
C. 66
D. 98
E. 114

80

4. The function f is defined by
$f(x) = a \sin bx - c$, where a, b, and c are positive real numbers. What is the minimum possible value of $f(x)$?

   A. $-a$
   B. $-a - c$
   C. $a - c$
   D. $-b - c$
   E. $b - c$

5. For isosceles trapezoid $ABCD$ shown below, $AD = 18$ ft, $BC = 10$ ft, and $\angle D$ measures $67°$. Which of the following represents the height, in feet, of $ABCD$?

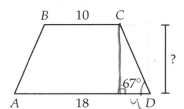

   A. $4 \cos 67°$
   B. $4 \tan 67°$
   C. $\dfrac{4}{\tan 67°}$
   D. $10 \sin 67°$
   E. $10 \tan 67°$

   $\tan 67 = \dfrac{x}{4}$

   $x = 4$

6. If $\csc A = 1.8$, what is the value of $\sin A$?

   A. $\dfrac{2}{3}$
   B. $\dfrac{4}{5}$
   C. $\dfrac{5}{9}$
   D. $\sqrt{2.24}$
   E. $\dfrac{1}{\sqrt{2.24}}$

   $\dfrac{1}{1.8}$ $\dfrac{a}{15}$

7. To approximate the width of a marsh, a surveyor walks 240 meters from point B to point C in the figure below. During the walk, the surveyor sights point A and determines that $\angle B$ is a right angle and $\angle C$ measures $37°$. How wide, in meters, is the marsh?

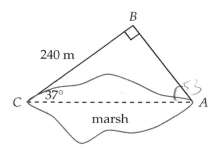

marsh

   A. $240 \sin 37°$
   B. $240 \cos 37°$
   C. $\dfrac{240}{\sin 37°}$
   D. $\dfrac{240}{\cos 37°}$
   E. $\dfrac{240}{\tan 37°}$

   $\cos 37 = \dfrac{240}{x}$

   $x = \dfrac{240}{\cos}$

8. Two angles are coterminal. If the measure of the first angle is $\dfrac{19}{4}\pi$ radians, which of the following could be the measure of the second angle?

   A. $45°$
   B. $90°$
   C. $135°$
   D. $180°$
   E. $225°$

66

9. A sailboat leaves shore at a bearing of 64° and travels from point A to point B in the figure below. The captain wants to know how far the boat is from shore. From the sighting of a landmark at point C, it is determined that the boat is 8 kilometers downstream from point A. Which of the following expressions gives the boat's distance from shore, in kilometers, represented by the length of $\overline{BC}$?

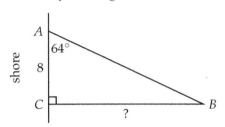

A. $8\sin 64°$
B. $8\cos 64°$
C. $8\tan 64°$
D. $\dfrac{8}{\sin 64°}$
E. $\dfrac{8}{\tan 64°}$

$\tan 64 = \dfrac{x}{9}$

$x = ta$

10. In $\triangle CDE$, $\angle C$ is a right angle, $CE = 12$ units, and $\tan\angle D = \dfrac{4}{5}$. What is the area of $\triangle CDE$, in square units?

A. 57.6
B. 90
C. 115.2
D. 120
E. 180

11. If $\sin\theta = -\dfrac{1}{4}$, what is the value of $\cos 2\theta$?

$\left(\text{Note: } (\sin\theta)^2 = \dfrac{1-\cos 2\theta}{2}\right)$

A. 0
B. $\dfrac{1}{8}$
C. $\dfrac{5}{8}$
D. $\dfrac{7}{8}$
E. $\dfrac{3}{4}$

$2(\sin\theta)^2 = 1 - \cos 2\theta$

$2(\sin\theta)^2 - 1 = -\cos 2\theta$

12. A carpenter needs to use a ladder to climb a wall. The ladder is 18 feet long and the wall is 13 feet high, as shown in the figure below. If the carpenter positions the ladder so that it just reaches the top of the wall, which of the following expressions gives the measure of the angle from the ground to the ladder?

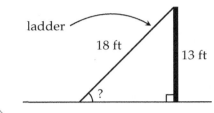

A. $\arcsin\left(\dfrac{13}{18}\right)$
B. $\arcsin\left(\dfrac{\sqrt{155}}{18}\right)$
C. $\arccos\left(\dfrac{13}{18}\right)$
D. $\arctan\left(\dfrac{13}{18}\right)$
E. $\arctan\left(\dfrac{18}{13}\right)$

13. Triangle $\triangle ABC$ is shown below with the given side lengths in meters. Which of the following gives the area, in square meters, of $\triangle ABC$?

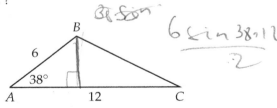

A. $36\sin 38°$
B. $36\cos 38°$
C. $36\tan 38°$
D. $72\sin 38°$
E. $72\cos 38°$

$\sin 38 = \dfrac{y}{6}$

$6\sin 38°$

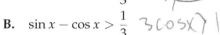

14. Let θ be the degree angle measure that satisfies $\sin\theta = \dfrac{3}{5}$ for $0° \leq \theta \leq 180°$. What are all possible values of $\tan\theta$?

   A. $-\dfrac{3}{4}$ only

   B. $\dfrac{3}{4}$ only

   C. $-\dfrac{3}{4}$ and $\dfrac{3}{4}$

   D. $\dfrac{4}{3}$ only

   E. $-\dfrac{4}{3}$ and $\dfrac{4}{3}$

15. After striking the surface of a piece of glass, a beam of light traveled 8.4 millimeters through the glass at an angle of refraction of θ, as shown in the figure below. The glass is 5.2 millimeters thick. Which of the following expressions gives the measure of the angle of refraction?

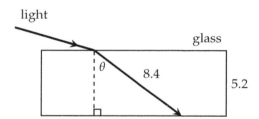

   A. $\sin^{-1}\left(\dfrac{5.2}{8.4}\right)$

   B. $\sin^{-1}\left(\dfrac{8.4}{5.2}\right)$

   C. $\tan^{-1}\left(\dfrac{5.2}{8.4}\right)$

   D. $\tan^{-1}\left(\dfrac{8.4}{5.2}\right)$

   E. $\cos^{-1}\left(\dfrac{5.2}{8.4}\right)$

16. For all values of x such that $\sin x > 0$ and $\tan x > 0$, which of the following inequalities is equivalent to $\sin x > \dfrac{1}{3}\tan x$?

   A. $\sin x + \cos x > \dfrac{1}{3}$

   B. $\sin x - \cos x > \dfrac{1}{3}$

   C. $\dfrac{\sin^2 x}{\cos x} < 3$

   D. $\cos x > \dfrac{1}{3}$

   E. $\cos x < 3$

17. In the figure below, the side lengths of a triangle are given in inches. Which of the following equations can be used to find the angle measure θ ?
(Note: The law of cosines states that for any triangle, $c^2 = a^2 + b^2 - 2ab\cos C$, where a, b, and c are the lengths of the sides and C is the measure of the angle opposite the side of length c.)

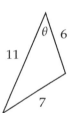

   A. $\cos\theta = \dfrac{6}{11}$

   B. $\tan\theta = \dfrac{7}{6}$

   C. $6^2 = 7^2 + 11^2 - 2(7)(11)\cos\theta$

   D. $7^2 = 6^2 + 11^2 - 2(6)(11)\cos\theta$

   E. $11^2 = 6^2 + 7^2 - 2(6)(7)\cos\theta$

18. For all x such that $\tan x \neq 0$, the expression $\dfrac{\sin^2 x \cdot \sec x}{\tan x}$ is equivalent to which of the following?

   (Note: $\sec x = \dfrac{1}{\cos x}$ and $\tan x = \dfrac{\sin x}{\cos x}$)

   A. $\cos x$

   B. $\sin x$

   C. $\sin^3 x$

   D. $\cos x \cdot \sin^2 x$

   E. $\sin x \cdot \cos^2 x$

19. The domain of the function
$f(x) = 2\sin(3x + 5) - 1$ is all real numbers.
Which of the following gives the range of
$f(x)$?

A. $-1 \le f(x) \le 1$
B. $-1 \le f(x) \le 3$
C. $-2 \le f(x) \le 2$
D. $-3 \le f(x) \le 1$
E. All real numbers

[handwritten: 2) 8]
[handwritten: 2   1]

20. The expression $2\cos^2 x - 2\sin^2 x$ is
equivalent to which of the following?
(Note: $\cos(x + y) = \cos x \cos y - \sin x \sin y$)

A. $\cos 2x$
B. $2\cos 2x$
C. $4\cos 2x$
D. $\cos x^2$
E. $2\cos x^2$

[handwritten: $2\left(\cos^2 x - \sin^2 x\right)$]
[handwritten: $\cos(2x) = \cos^2 x - \sin^2 x$]

21. In $\triangle FGH$, shown below, a side length is
given in inches and angle measures are as
marked. Which of the following is an
expression for the length, in inches, of $\overline{FH}$?

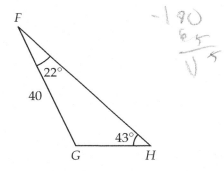

[handwritten: -180 / 65 / $\overline{15}$]

(Note: The law of sines states that for a
triangle $\triangle ABC$ with sides of lengths a, b, and
c opposite their respective angles,
$$\frac{\sin \angle A}{a} = \frac{\sin \angle B}{b} = \frac{\sin \angle C}{c}.)$$

A. $\dfrac{40\sin 22°}{\sin 43°}$
B. $\dfrac{40\sin 22°}{\sin 115°}$
C. $\dfrac{40\sin 43°}{\sin 22°}$
D. $\dfrac{40\sin 115°}{\sin 22°}$
E. $\dfrac{40\sin 115°}{\sin 43°}$

[handwritten right column:]
[$2(\cos(2x))$]
[$\dfrac{40\sin 115}{\sin 43}$]
[$\dfrac{\sin 43}{40} = \dfrac{\sin 115}{FH}$]
[$\dfrac{\sin 43}{40} = \dfrac{\sin 22}{GH}$]
[$\sin 43 \cdot GH = 40\sin 22$]
[$\dfrac{40\sin 22}{\sin 43}$]
[$\dfrac{\sin 22}{GH} = \dfrac{\sin 43}{40}$]
[$\dfrac{40\sin 22 = GH\sin 43}{\sin 43}$]

23

Permutations & Probability

Answers start on page 136.

1. A fruit basket contains 2 apples, 4 oranges, and 9 bananas. One piece of fruit will be randomly selected from the basket. What is the probability that the selected piece of fruit is NOT a banana?

   A. $\dfrac{2}{3}$

   B. $\dfrac{2}{5}$

   C. $\dfrac{3}{5}$

   D. $\dfrac{2}{15}$

   E. $\dfrac{4}{15}$

2. There are 8 boys and 12 girls in a class. If the teacher will pick one boy and one girl to lead a class discussion, how many different pairs of students are possible?

   A. 20
   B. 56
   C. 77
   D. 96
   E. 132

3. A bin contains only 10 footballs, 4 basketballs, 6 baseballs, and n tennis balls. What is the probability that a randomly chosen ball from the bin is a tennis ball?

   A. $\dfrac{1}{20}$

   B. $\dfrac{n}{20}$

   C. $\dfrac{1}{n}$

   D. $\dfrac{1}{n+20}$

   E. $\dfrac{n}{n+20}$

4. A drawer contains 80 pens, some of which are black and some of which are blue. The probability of randomly choosing a black pen from the drawer is $\dfrac{3}{5}$. How many blue pens are in the drawer?

   A. 24
   B. 32
   C. 40
   D. 48
   E. 56

70

5. A restaurant offers a dinner menu that consists of 3 appetizers, 4 entrees, and 4 desserts. How many different dinners are possible for a customer who orders exactly 1 appetizer, 1 entree, and 1 dessert?

   A. 3
   B. 11
   C. 24
   D. 48
   E. 990

6. There are 5 green beads and 23 yellow beads in a container. Kayla will draw two beads from the container at random and without replacement. Which of the following expressions gives the probability that Kayla will draw 2 green beads?

   A. $\dfrac{5}{28} \cdot \dfrac{4}{27}$

   B. $\dfrac{5}{28} + \dfrac{4}{27}$

   C. $\dfrac{5}{28} \cdot \dfrac{4}{28}$

   D. $\dfrac{5}{28} \cdot \dfrac{5}{28}$

   E. $\dfrac{5}{28} + \dfrac{5}{28}$

7. Of the marbles in a bowl, 18 are green and the rest are red. The probability of randomly choosing a green marble from the bowl is $\dfrac{3}{5}$. How many red marbles are in the bowl?

   A. 9
   B. 12
   C. 15
   D. 18
   E. 21

8. In how many different ways can 6 people sitting in a row of seats be ordered?

   A. 6
   B. 21
   C. 36
   D. 720
   E. 46,656

9. If a number is chosen at random from the set $\{-3, -2, -1, 0, 1, 2, 3\}$, what is the probability that the chosen number will be a solution to both $3x + 5 < 14$ and $2x - 3 > -5$?

   A. $\dfrac{3}{7}$

   B. $\dfrac{4}{7}$

   C. $\dfrac{5}{7}$

   D. $\dfrac{6}{7}$

   E. 1

10. A deck of cards contains 24 red cards and 36 blue cards. How many blue cards must be removed from the deck so that the probability of randomly drawing a blue card is $\dfrac{2}{5}$?

    A. 12
    B. 18
    C. 20
    D. 24
    E. 27

11. A number is randomly chosen from the set $\{1, 2, 3\}$ and a second number is randomly chosen from the set $\{4, 5, 6\}$. What is the probability that the sum of the two chosen numbers is 6?

    A. $\dfrac{1}{2}$

    B. $\dfrac{1}{3}$

    C. $\dfrac{1}{9}$

    D. $\dfrac{2}{9}$

    E. $\dfrac{4}{9}$

24

Data & Statistics

Answers start on page 138.

1. An airline requested the food and drink preferences of all the passengers on a certain flight. The results are shown in the table below. How many passengers prefer water with their meal?

Drink	Food	
	Chicken	Vegetarian
Water	56	24
Soda	32	8

   A. 24
   B. 40
   C. 56
   D. 80
   E. 88

2. The average of 8 numbers is 68. The average of the first 6 of those numbers is 65. What is the average of the 7th and 8th numbers?

   A. 68
   B. 71
   C. 74
   D. 77
   E. 154

3. The table below gives the word count distribution for 24 essays. Which of the following could be the median word count of the essays?

Word Count	Frequency
500—600	3
601—700	2
701—800	4
801—900	8
901—1000	7

   A. 540
   B. 650
   C. 760
   D. 870
   E. 980

4. The table below shows data from a 2001 study on media consumption.

Primary Source of News	Number of people in the sample
Magazines	30
Newspapers	25
Television	45
Websites	15
Radio	65

If a circle graph were used to show the information above, what would be the measure of the central angle of the sector representing those whose primary source of news is television?

A. 30°
B. 50°
C. 60°
D. 80°
E. 90°

5. There are 5 cookies in a jar. The average sugar content of the cookies is 9 grams. A sixth cookie has 18 grams of sugar and is added to the jar. What is the new average sugar content of the cookies in the jar, to the nearest 0.1 grams?

A. 9.5
B. 10.0
C. 10.5
D. 11.0
E. 11.5

Use the following information to answer questions 6–7.

In the game of chess, the player with the white pieces moves first and the player with black pieces moves second. The players continue taking turns until one player "checkmates" the other with the last move. The table below gives the results of a chess match consisting of 7 games that all finished with checkmate.

	Winner	Number of moves
Game 1	White	21
Game 2	Black	24
Game 3	Black	52
Game 4	White	35
Game 5	Black	18
Game 6	White	47
Game 7	Black	26

6. What was the median number of moves per game in the chess match?

A. 21
B. 24
C. 25
D. 26
E. 35

7. A total of 132 moves were made in the first 4 games. How many of these moves were made by the player with the white pieces?

A. 56
B. 65
C. 66
D. 67
E. 76

8. The graph below shows the distance, d miles, John is from his house t minutes after he starts jogging. Which of the following statements could describe what John did at $t = 30$?

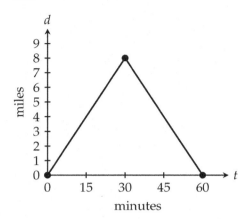

A. He turned around to jog back to his house.
B. He started jogging at a faster speed.
C. He stopped to rest on a bench.
D. He slowed down to a walk.
E. He arrived back at his house.

9. The equation $y = ax + b$, where a and b are real numbers, represents the line of best fit for the points shown in the standard (x, y) coordinate plane below. Which of the following best approximates the value of a ?

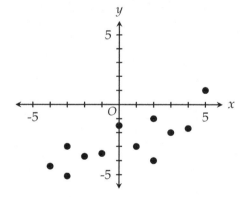

A. -3
B. $-\dfrac{1}{2}$
C. 0
D. $\dfrac{1}{2}$
E. 2

10. The graph below shows how many movies were produced by a studio each year from 2001 to 2006. In which year did the studio produce 50% more movies than it did the previous year?

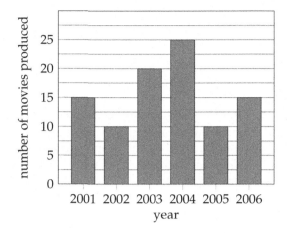

A. 2002
B. 2003
C. 2004
D. 2005
E. 2006

11. The elements of a data set are shown in the stem-and-leaf plot below. What is the mode of the data set?

Stem	Leaf
3	5 5 6 7
4	2 7 7
5	1 3 3 3 4 9

(Note: A stem of 3 and a leaf of 5 represents the number 35.)

A. 24
B. 35
C. 47
D. 53
E. 59

74

12. Nancy opens 11 different bags of chips, counts the number of chips in each bag, and finds that the median number of chips in a bag is 38. She then draws a bar graph to represent this data. Which of the following could be Nancy's bar graph?

A.
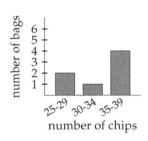

B.
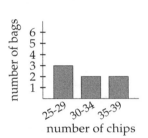

C.
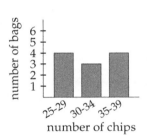

D.
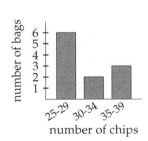

E.
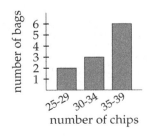

13. Casey added new coins to his collection by traveling to different countries during a 4 month period. The points on the graph below show the total number of coins in his collection at the end of each month.

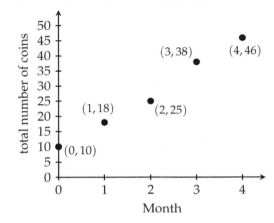

How many coins did Casey add to his collection in Month 3?

A. 8
B. 13
C. 25
D. 28
E. 38

14. The table below shows the height h, in feet, of a rocket t seconds after it was launched. What was the average speed of the rocket, in feet per second, from $t = 1$ to $t = 4$?

t	h
0	0
1	8
2	20
3	36
4	62
5	108

A. 9
B. 12
C. 13.5
D. 15.5
E. 18

15. A data set contains the 5 elements listed below. Which of the following gives the difference between the mean and the median of the data set?

$$x, \; x+2, \; x+4, \; x+6, \; x+8$$

A. 0
B. 2
C. $x+4$
D. $2x+8$
E. $4x+16$

16. A data set has 5 different positive integers, three of which are 1, 2, and 6. The mean of the data set is 5 and the median of the data set is 6. What is the largest integer in the data set?

A. 7
B. 8
C. 9
D. 10
E. 15

17. Each element in a data set containing 50 elements is multiplied by -1 to generate a second data set containing 50 elements. Each of the 50 elements in the second data set is increased by 5 to generate a third data set of 50 elements. The median of the third data set is y. Which of the following expressions is equal to the median of the original data set?

A. $-y+5$
B. $-y-5$
C. $y+5$
D. $y-5$
E. $-\dfrac{y}{5}$

18. The median of a list of 60 whole numbers is 75. None of the numbers in the list are equal to 75, and 20% of the numbers in the list are equal to or less than 72. How many numbers in the list are equal to 73 or 74?

A. 12
B. 18
C. 24
D. 36
E. 48

19. Amy and Bob have different exercise routines. Amy first bikes up a hill at a constant speed. Once she reaches the top, she then continuously speeds up until she reaches the bottom of the hill. Bob bikes at a constant speed throughout his routine. Which of the following graphs best illustrates Amy and Bob's respective exercise routines?
(Note: A stands for Amy and B stands for Bob.)

A.

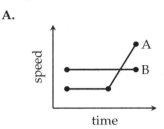

B.

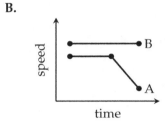

C.

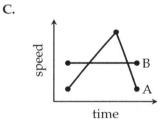

D.

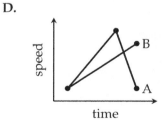

E.

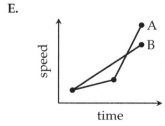

25

Logarithms

Answers start on page 140.

1. What is the value of $\log_5\left(\frac{1}{25}\right)$?

    A. -5

    B. -2

    C. $-\frac{1}{2}$

    D. $\frac{1}{5}$

    E. $\frac{1}{2}$

2. For what value of x does $\log_2(x-3) = 1$

    A.   1

    B.   2

    C.   3

    D.   5

    E.   16

3. Which of the following values of x satisfies the equation $\log_8 x = -\frac{2}{3}$?

    A. -4

    B. $\frac{3}{16}$

    C. $\frac{1}{4}$

    D.   4

    E.   12

4. Given that $\log_a 5 = -1$, what is the value of a ?

    A. $-\frac{1}{5}$

    B. $\frac{1}{5}$

    C. -5

    D.   6

    E.   25

5. What is the value of x if $\log_4 x - \log_4 2 = 3$?

    A.   16

    B.   32

    C.   64

    D.   66

    E.   128

6. If $\log_3 7 = k$, what is the value of $\log_3 49$ in terms of k ?

    A. k^2

    B. $2k$

    C. $7k$

    D. $k+7$

    E. $k+14$

7. If $x = \log_4 3$, what is the value of 4^{x+1} ?

    A.   4
    B.   7
    C.   12
    D.   64
    E.   256

8. What is the value of x in the equation
$\log_7 x = \log_3 18 - \log_3 2$?

    A.   16
    B.   36
    C.   49
    D.   128
    E.   343

9. Whenever a and b are positive real numbers, which of the following expressions is equivalent to $\log_2 a - 2\log_5 b + \log_2(3a)$?

    A. $\log_2\left(\dfrac{3a^2}{b^2}\right)$

    B. $\log_2(4a) - \log_5(2b)$
    C. $\log_2(4a) - \log_5(b^2)$
    D. $\log_2(3a^2) - \log_5(2b)$
    E. $\log_2(3a^2) - \log_5(b^2)$

10. If $2^x = 5$ and $2^y = 7$, then $x + y = ?$

    A. $\sqrt{35}$
    B.   6
    C. $\log_2 12$
    D. $\log_2 35$
    E. $(\log_2 5)(\log_2 7)$

26

A Mix of Algebra Topics

Answers start on page 141.

1. Kyle cuts a block of wood weighing 72 ounces into two pieces. The heavier piece weighs 20 more ounces than the smaller piece. What is the weight, in ounces, of the smaller piece of wood?

   A. 21
   B. 26
   C. 41
   D. 46
   E. 52

2. The number of radioactive atoms, n, present in a chemical compound after t years is given by $n = 5,000e^{-0.3t}$, where $e \approx 2.72$. Which of the following is closest to the number of radioactive atoms present in the compound after 4 years?

   A. 1,505
   B. 2,318
   C. 3,114
   D. 3,967
   E. 14,816

3. Casey keeps 84 pebbles that are either red, black, or purple in a jar. He takes each one out of the jar and find that there are 9 more black pebbles than red and 12 more purple pebbles than black. How many purple pebbles does Casey have?

   A. 18
   B. 21
   C. 24
   D. 27
   E. 39

Use the following information to answer questions 4–6.

The amount of money in a bank account can be modeled by the formula $A = P(1 + r)^t$, where P is the dollar amount of the initial deposit; r is the annual interest rate, expressed as a decimal; and A is the total dollar amount in the account at the end of t years.

4. Which of the following equations gives r in terms of the other variables in the formula?

   A. $r = 1 - \sqrt[t]{\dfrac{A}{P}}$

   B. $r = 1 + \sqrt[t]{\dfrac{A}{P}}$

   C. $r = \sqrt[t]{\dfrac{A}{P}} - 1$

   D. $r = \dfrac{\sqrt[t]{A}}{P} - 1$

   E. $r = t \log\left(\dfrac{A}{P}\right) - 1$

5. Kimberly makes an initial deposit of $10,000 into a bank account that earns 5% annual interest. According to the model, what is the total amount of money, to the nearest dollar, in Kimberly's account at the end of 6 years?

   A. $12,727
   B. $13,401
   C. $14,368
   D. $14,889
   E. $15,112

6. Jeffrey opens up a bank account that earns 4% annual interest and makes an initial deposit. He plans to withdraw all the money in the account once the total amount is double his initial deposit. According to the model, which of the following expressions gives the number of years Jeffrey will have to wait before he can make his withdrawal?

   A. $\dfrac{1}{0.04}$

   B. $\dfrac{2}{1 + 0.04}$

   C. $\sqrt{\dfrac{2}{1 + 0.04}}$

   D. $\dfrac{\log 2}{\log(1 + 0.04)}$

   E. $\dfrac{\log 200}{\log(104)}$

7. A retail store sells tee-shirts in 3 different sizes: small, medium, and large. Last week, customers bought 3 times as many large tee-shirts as small tee-shirts, and customers bought 5 times as many medium tee-shirts as small tee-shirts. Last week, the store sold 720 tee-shirts. How many of these 720 were small tee-shirts?

   A. 80
   B. 90
   C. 120
   D. 180
   E. 240

8. Mark and Tracy are teachers who grade a total of 210 essays per semester. Each semester, Tracy grades $2\dfrac{1}{2}$ times the number of essays Mark grades. How many essays will Tracy grade over a period of 3 semesters?

   A. 180
   B. 252
   C. 450
   D. 525
   E. 630

9. During the grand opening, a restaurant sold discounted appetizers to attract customers to its entrees. The restaurant earned $6 on each entree sold and lost $2 on each appetizer sold. The restaurant sold twice as many entrees as appetizers for a total of $1,200 in net earnings. How many entrees did the restaurant sell during its grand opening?

    A. 120
    B. 150
    C. 240
    D. 300
    E. 600

10. An urban planner is designing a public garden. Because of city regulations, the length of the garden, l meters, depends on the width, w meters. The equation $l = 60 - 2w$, where $0 < w < 30$, gives the relationship between l and w. If the planner wants the garden to have the maximum possible area, how wide must the garden be, in meters?

    A. 12
    B. 15
    C. 18
    D. 20
    E. 24

11. Jamie buys two varieties of protein bars: Protein Bar A, which contains 15 grams of protein, and Protein Bar B, which contains 18 grams of protein. The shaded region in the coordinate plane below gives the possible quantities of Protein Bar A and Protein Bar B Jamie can buy each week given his budget. Within these constraints, what is the maximum possible amount of protein, in grams, Jamie can consume from 1 week's supply of protein bars?

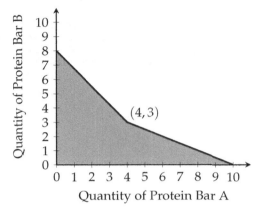

    A. 114
    B. 120
    C. 144
    D. 150
    E. 156

27

Miscellaneous Topics I

Answers start on page 144.

1. An arithmetic sequence has a first term of 7 and a common difference of 4. What is the 5th term in the sequence?

   A. -9
   B. 23
   C. 27
   D. 32
   E. 39

2. The second term of a geometric sequence is -9, and the third term is -3. What is the first term?

   A. -27
   B. -18
   C. -15
   D. -1
   E. 3

3. The first 3 terms of a geometric sequence are 9, 12, 16. What is the 4th term of the sequence?

   A. $\dfrac{20}{3}$
   B. 18
   C. 20
   D. 21
   E. $\dfrac{64}{3}$

4. A row of bricks is shown below. Each brick is 8 inches wide and separated from the next brick by 1 inch of cement. If the row of bricks must start with a brick and end with a brick, which of the following could be the total length, in inches, of the row of bricks?

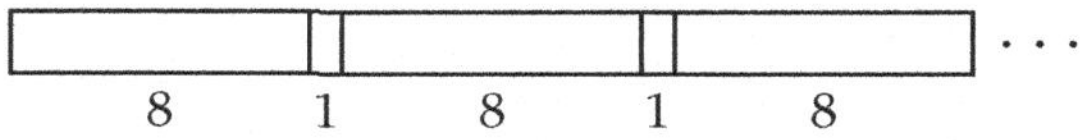

   A. 500
   B. 501
   C. 502
   D. 503
   E. 504

5. A two digit number XY, where X and Y are digits, is reversed to form the two digit number YX. If the difference between the two numbers is 36 and $X + Y = 10$, what is the product of digit X and digit Y ?

   A. 9
   B. 16
   C. 21
   D. 24
   E. 25

6. A cafe asked 150 customers whether they had bought coffee or tea in the past month. Of the 150 customers, 98 had bought coffee, 76 had bought tea, and 44 had bought both coffee and tea. Of the 150 customers, how many had bought neither coffee nor tea?

   A. 6
   B. 8
   C. 20
   D. 30
   E. 68

7. The 5th term of an arithmetic sequence is 7, and the 10th term is 13. What is the sum of the first 3 terms of the sequence?

   A. 5.6
   B. 6.6
   C. 7.8
   D. 10.2
   E. 12

8. At a deli, ticket numbers are different positive integers assigned to customers by using the rule that no combination of assigned ticket numbers can sum to another ticket number. If 6 customers have received ticket numbers and the largest ticket number among these is x, what is the smallest possible value of x ?

   A. 16
   B. 28
   C. 32
   D. 36
   E. 40

9. A state's department of education gave 180 middle school teachers an exam to determine which subjects they were qualified to teach. The results are shown in the Venn diagram below for math, science, and history. Based on the results of the exam, what percent of the teachers were qualified to teach exactly 1 subject?

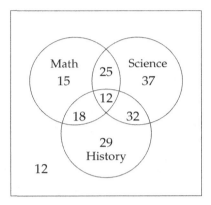

   A. 40%
   B. 45%
   C. 50%
   D. 55%
   E. 60%

10. In a certain number sequence, each term after the first term is obtained by adding 4 to the previous term and multiplying that sum by 2. The 3rd term in the sequence is 48. What is the 1st term?

    A. 4
    B. 6
    C. 9
    D. 11
    E. 20

11. The sum of an infinite geometric series is given by $\dfrac{a}{1-r}$, where a is the first term and r is the common ratio between 0 and 1. A certain infinite geometric series has a sum of 96 and a common ratio of 0.25. What is the third term of this series?

    A. 4.5
    B. 18
    C. 72
    D. 72.5
    E. 95.5

12. Consecutive numbers starting from 1 are arranged in rows to form the triangular pattern shown below. What is the first number of the 15th row?

$$1$$
$$2 \quad 3 \quad 4$$
$$5 \quad 6 \quad 7 \quad 8 \quad 9$$
$$10 \quad 11 \quad 12 \quad 13 \quad 14 \quad 15 \quad 16$$
$$\vdots$$

A. 196
B. 197
C. 198
D. 199
E. 200

13. Nine congruent equilateral triangles were used to form an outer triangle with 3 levels, as shown below. How many congruent equilateral triangles must be used to form an outer triangle with 11 levels?

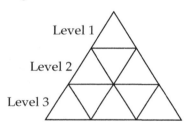

A. 99
B. 100
C. 110
D. 111
E. 121

28

Miscellaneous Topics II

Answers start on page 146.

1. All of the following figures in the standard (x, y) coordinate plane are symmetric across both the x-axis and the y-axis EXCEPT:

C.

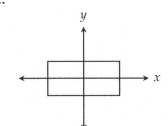

A.

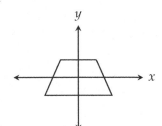

B.

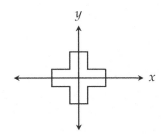

D.

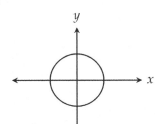

E.

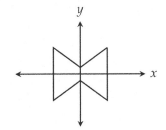

2. $\begin{bmatrix} a & b \\ c & d \end{bmatrix} + \begin{bmatrix} -a & b \\ 0 & 1 \end{bmatrix} = ?$

   A. $\begin{bmatrix} 0 & 0 \\ c & d+1 \end{bmatrix}$

   B. $\begin{bmatrix} 0 & 2b \\ c & d+1 \end{bmatrix}$

   C. $\begin{bmatrix} 0 & b^2 \\ c & d \end{bmatrix}$

   D. $\begin{bmatrix} 2a & 0 \\ c & d-1 \end{bmatrix}$

   E. $\begin{bmatrix} -a^2 & b^2 \\ 0 & d \end{bmatrix}$

3. At a clothing store, if a tie does not cost more than 50 dollars, then it is not on display. If Carl bought a tie that was on display at the store today, then which of the following may be logically concluded?

   A. Carl spent at most 40 dollars on the tie.
   B. Carl spent less than 50 dollars on the tie.
   C. Carl spent exactly 50 dollars on the tie.
   D. Carl spent more than 50 dollars on the tie.
   E. Carl spent at least 60 dollars on the tie.

4. The matrix $A = \begin{bmatrix} 6 & -3 \\ 1 & 1 \end{bmatrix}$ and

   $A + B = \begin{bmatrix} 4 & 2 \\ -1 & 8 \end{bmatrix}$. Which of the following gives matrix B ?

   A. $\begin{bmatrix} -2 & -5 \\ 2 & 7 \end{bmatrix}$

   B. $\begin{bmatrix} -2 & 5 \\ -2 & 7 \end{bmatrix}$

   C. $\begin{bmatrix} 2 & -5 \\ 2 & -7 \end{bmatrix}$

   D. $\begin{bmatrix} 10 & -1 \\ 0 & 9 \end{bmatrix}$

   E. $\begin{bmatrix} 24 & -6 \\ -1 & 8 \end{bmatrix}$

5. What is the <u>least</u> number of marbles needed to place 3 marbles on each line segment of the figure below?

   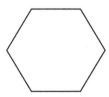

   A. 9
   B. 12
   C. 15
   D. 18
   E. 21

6. How many right angles does the right rectangular prism shown below have?

   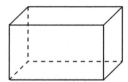

   A. 8
   B. 12
   C. 16
   D. 24
   E. 32

7. How many rectangles are in the figure below?

   A. 5
   B. 7
   C. 8
   D. 10
   E. 12

8. All of the following could be the shape of the intersection of a plane and a right circular cone EXCEPT:

   A. a point
   B. a line
   C. a circle
   D. a triangle
   E. a rectangle

9. The *determinant* of a 2×2 matrix $\begin{bmatrix} a & b \\ c & d \end{bmatrix}$ is given by $ad - bc$. If the matrix $\begin{bmatrix} x & 3 \\ 5 & (x+4) \end{bmatrix}$ has a determinant of 6, what are all possible values of x?

A. -7 and 3
B. -4 and 0
C. -4 and 8
D. -3 and 7
E. $-\sqrt{21}$ and $\sqrt{21}$

10. A ticket agent made the true statement below.

If the box office is closed, then the event is sold out.

Which of the following statements is logically equivalent to the ticket agent's statement?

A. The event is sold out if and only if the box office is closed.
B. If the event is not sold out, then the box office is not closed.
C. If the box office is not closed, then the event is not sold out.
D. If the event is sold out, then the box office is closed.
E. The box office is closed, or the event is sold out.

11. The graph in the standard (x, y) coordinate plane below is determined by one of the following equations. Which one?

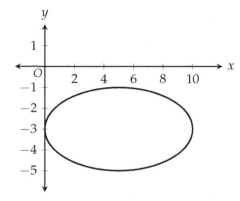

A. $\dfrac{(x+5)^2}{10} + \dfrac{(y-3)^2}{4} = 1$

B. $\dfrac{(x+5)^2}{25} + \dfrac{(y-3)^2}{4} = 1$

C. $\dfrac{(x-5)^2}{5} + \dfrac{(y+3)^2}{2} = 1$

D. $\dfrac{(x-5)^2}{10} + \dfrac{(y+3)^2}{4} = 1$

E. $\dfrac{(x-5)^2}{25} + \dfrac{(y+3)^2}{4} = 1$

12. If $X = \begin{bmatrix} 1 & 1 \\ 1 & 1 \end{bmatrix}$ and the matrix product XY is defined, which of the following CANNOT be matrix Y?

A. $\begin{bmatrix} 4 \\ 3 \end{bmatrix}$

B. $\begin{bmatrix} 0 & 0 \\ 0 & 0 \end{bmatrix}$

C. $\begin{bmatrix} 5 & -6 \\ 8 & 2 \end{bmatrix}$

D. $\begin{bmatrix} 7 & 1 \\ 3 & 4 \\ 4 & 9 \end{bmatrix}$

E. $\begin{bmatrix} 3 & 2 & 2 \\ -1 & 8 & 6 \end{bmatrix}$

13. Which of the following (x, y) pairs satisfies the matrix equation below?

$$\begin{bmatrix} x & 0 \\ 1 & 7 \end{bmatrix} + \begin{bmatrix} -5 & 1 \\ 0 & \frac{x}{3} \end{bmatrix} = \begin{bmatrix} y & 1 \\ 1 & y \end{bmatrix}$$

A. $(18, 13)$
B. $(9, 10)$
C. $(8, 3)$
D. $(6, 1)$
E. $(3, 8)$

14. The ellipse in the standard (x, y) coordinate plane below can be represented by one of the following equations. Which one?

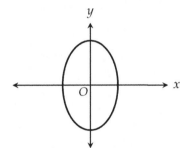

A. $\dfrac{x^2}{9} - \dfrac{y^2}{25} = 1$

B. $\dfrac{x^2}{9} + \dfrac{y^2}{25} = 1$

C. $\dfrac{x^2}{25} - \dfrac{y^2}{9} = 1$

D. $\dfrac{x^2}{25} + \dfrac{y^2}{9} = 1$

E. $(x - 5)^2 + (y - 3)^2 = 1$

29
Answers to the Exercises

Exercise 1: Absolute Value

1. $\boxed{B}$ $-4\,|-6| = -4\cdot 6 = -24$

2. $\boxed{C}$ If $x \le -3$, then $x+3$ is always negative or zero. Taking its absolute value would then be equivalent to multiplying by -1 (turning a negative into a positive), giving $-x-3$. A more concrete way of solving this problem would be to make up a number for x. If we let $x = -5$, then $|x+3| = |-5+3| = |-2| = 2$. The only answer choice that gives 2 when $x = -5$ is $-x-3$.

3. $\boxed{C}$ $(x-y)^2 - |x-y| = (5-7)^2 - |5-7| = (-2)^2 - |-2| = 4 - 2 = 2$.

4. $\boxed{D}$ We have two cases. When $5-y = 10$, $y = -5$. When $5-y = -10$, $y = 15$. The two possible values of y are -5 and 15.

5. $\boxed{D}$ We try out different numbers. When $x = 5$, $|x-3| = 2$. The only answer choices that give 2 when $x = 5$ are A and D. Let's try a negative number. When $x = -2$, $|x-3| = 5$. Between A and D, only D gives 5 when $x = -2$.

6. $\boxed{D}$ Let's make up a number for x. When $x = 5$, $|x|^2 = 25$. All of the answer choices give 25 when $x = 5$ except for D, which gives -25.

7. $\boxed{B}$ When y is positive, let's say 3, then $|y| - y = 3 - 3 = 0$. When y is negative, let's say -3, then $|y| - y = |-3| - (-3) = 3 + 3 = 6$. From here, it's easy to see that the result is sometimes positive.

8. $\boxed{D}$ Let $x = 3$ and $y = 5$. Then $|x-y| = |3-5| = |-2| = 2$. The only answer choice that yields 2 when given our chosen values of x and y is D.

9. $\boxed{B}$ If we let $x = 2$, then $|x-3| + |3-x| = |2-3| + |3-2| = |-1| + |1| = 2$. The only answer choice that evaluates to 2 when $x = 2$ is B.

Exercise 2: Exponents & Radicals

1. $\boxed{C}$ Divide the coefficients and subtract the exponents: $\dfrac{6x^8}{3x^2} = 2x^6$

2. $\boxed{C}$ $x^{\frac{3}{2}} = (x^3)^{\frac{1}{2}} = \sqrt{x^3} = \sqrt{x \cdot x \cdot x} = x\sqrt{x}$

3. $\boxed{B}$ $(-2)^3 + (-2)^2 = -8 + 4 = -4$

4. $\boxed{C}$ Anything raised to the 0 power is 1.

5. $\boxed{D}$ Multiply the coefficients and add the exponents: $3n^{-2} \cdot 2n^{-3} = 6n^{-5} = \dfrac{6}{n^5}$

6. $\boxed{B}$ Divide the coefficients and subtract the exponents: $-\dfrac{20x^8y^4}{5x^2y} = -4x^6y^3$

7. $\boxed{D}$ Both x^2 and z^4 are guaranteed to be positive because of their even exponents. So for $x^2y^3z^4$ to be positive, only y must be positive. We don't know whether x and z are positive or negative. Therefore, the only answer choice that must be positive is x^2y.

8. $\boxed{B}$

$$(x^3)^4(x^2)^5 = (x^b)^2$$
$$x^{12} \cdot x^{10} = x^{2b}$$
$$x^{22} = x^{2b}$$
$$22 = 2b$$
$$b = 11$$

9. $\boxed{B}$ $\sqrt{(\sqrt{23})^2 - (\sqrt{5})^2} = \sqrt{23 - 5} = \sqrt{18} = \sqrt{3 \cdot 3 \cdot 2} = 3\sqrt{2}$

10. $\boxed{B}$ $2(a^3)^2 \cdot (2a^3)^2 = 2a^6 \cdot 2^2(a^3)^2 = 2a^6 \cdot 4a^6 = 8a^{12}$

11. $\boxed{E}$ The key is to get the same denominator. Multiply the left fraction by $\dfrac{\sqrt{a}}{\sqrt{a}}$ and the right fraction by $\dfrac{\sqrt{2}}{\sqrt{2}}$.

$$\sqrt{\frac{a}{2}} + \sqrt{\frac{2}{a}} = \frac{\sqrt{a}}{\sqrt{2}} + \frac{\sqrt{2}}{\sqrt{a}} = \left(\frac{\sqrt{a}}{\sqrt{2}} \cdot \frac{\sqrt{a}}{\sqrt{a}}\right) + \left(\frac{\sqrt{2}}{\sqrt{a}} \cdot \frac{\sqrt{2}}{\sqrt{2}}\right) = \frac{a}{\sqrt{2a}} + \frac{2}{\sqrt{2a}} = \frac{a+2}{\sqrt{2a}}$$

12. $\boxed{D}$ Given that x is the base on both sides, the exponents must be equal to each other, $k = 3j$, and since $j, k,$ and x are all positive, k must be even so that both the left and right hand sides of the equation are always positive.

Exercise 3: Manipulating and Solving Equations

1. $\boxed{D}$

$$\frac{b}{-3} - 2 = -10$$

$$\frac{b}{-3} = -8$$

$$b = 24$$

2. $\boxed{A}$ $(x-11)(x-3) = (8-11)(8-3) = (-3)(5) = -15$

3. $\boxed{D}$

$$x^2y = 4$$

$$x^2 = \frac{4}{y}$$

$$x = \sqrt{\frac{4}{y}} = \frac{\sqrt{4}}{\sqrt{y}} = \frac{2}{\sqrt{y}}$$

4. $\boxed{A}$ Multiply both sides by 6.

$$\frac{1}{3}(2x+1) = \frac{1}{2}(x-4)$$

$$2(2x+1) = 3(x-4)$$

$$4x + 2 = 3x - 12$$

$$x = -14$$

5. $\boxed{D}$

$$d = a\left(\frac{c+1}{24}\right)$$

$$d = 6\left(\frac{c+1}{24}\right)$$

$$d = \frac{c+1}{4}$$

$$4d = c + 1$$

$$4d - 1 = c$$

6. $\boxed{A}$

$$\frac{b}{a+1} = c$$
$$b = c(a+1)$$
$$b = ac + c$$
$$b - c = ac$$
$$\frac{b}{c} - 1 = a$$

7. $\boxed{C}$

$$2ax = 3 - bx$$
$$2ax + bx = 3$$
$$x(2a + b) = 3$$
$$x = \frac{3}{2a + b}$$

8. $\boxed{B}$

$$ab = ac + bc$$
$$ab - bc = ac$$
$$b(a - c) = ac$$
$$b = \frac{ac}{a - c}$$

9. $\boxed{C}$

$$A = A_0(1 + i)^t$$
$$\frac{A}{A_0} = (1 + i)^t$$
$$\sqrt[t]{\frac{A}{A_0}} = 1 + i$$
$$\sqrt[t]{\frac{A}{A_0}} - 1 = i$$

10. $\boxed{B}$ Since $b = d$, $c = \sqrt{d} = \sqrt{b}$, so A must be true. Since $b = d$, $b^2 = d^2$, so C must be true. Since $b = d$, $b = d = a^2$, so D must be true. Since $c = \sqrt{d}$, we can square both sides to get $c^2 = d$, so E must be true. However, a is not necessarily equal to c even though $a^2 = b = d = c^2$. For example, $a = -5$ and $c = 5$.

Exercise 4: Expressions

1. $\boxed{B}$ $b^2 - 8b + 16 = (b-4)(b-4) = (b-4)^2$

2. $\boxed{D}$ $a(b+c) + b(a+c) + c(a+b) = ab + ac + ab + bc + ac + bc = 2ab + 2bc + 2ac$

3. $\boxed{A}$ $-x^2y - xy^2 = -xy(x+y)$

4. $\boxed{C}$ $(3a - 4b)(5b + 2a) = 15ab + 6a^2 - 20b^2 - 8ab = 6a^2 + 7ab - 20b^2$

5. $\boxed{E}$ It takes $\dfrac{4}{3}$ cups of water to make 1 pizza, so $\dfrac{4}{3}x$ cups of water are required to make x pizzas. It takes $\dfrac{5}{4}$ cups of water to make 1 cake, so $\dfrac{5}{4}y$ cups of water are required to make y cakes. The total number of cups of water required to make everything is $\dfrac{4}{3}x + \dfrac{5}{4}y$.

6. $\boxed{C}$ $4x^2 + 2x - 6 = 2(2x^2 + x - 3) = 2(x-1)(2x+3)$

7. $\boxed{D}$ $(x+2)^2 - 4x - 5 = (x+2)(x+2) - 4x - 5 = (x^2 + 2x + 2x + 4) - 4x - 5 = x^2 - 1 = (x+1)(x-1)$

8. $\boxed{A}$ $\dfrac{(x+4)^2}{x^2 - 16} = \dfrac{(x+4)^2}{(x+4)(x-4)} = \dfrac{x+4}{x-4}$

9. $\boxed{D}$ Factoring the denominators, we get $\dfrac{1}{3(x-2)} + \dfrac{1}{2(x-2)^2}$. The two fractions have a $(x-2)$ in common but because the second fraction has two of them, $(x-2)^2$, we'll need two in our least common denominator. When things are in common, you go with the highest power. We'll also need one factor of "3" and one factor of "2". Putting everything together, our least common denominator is $3 \cdot 2 \cdot (x-2)^2 = 6(x-2)^2$.

10. $\boxed{E}$ The x burgers cost bx dollars. The total number of additional condiments is xy and they cost a total of cxy dollars. Altogether, Michael's order cost $bx + cxy$ dollars. Finally, the change he gets back is $30 - (bx + cxy)$.

Exercise 5: Numbers and Operations

1. $\boxed{E}$ Since $\frac{m}{12} = \frac{1}{4}$, $m = 3$. Finally, $m \times 12 = 3 \times 12 = 36$. By the way, you don't need algebra for this question if you can immediately see that $3 \div 12 = \frac{1}{4}$.

2. $\boxed{B}$ We should assign one jellybean each to the two jars that contain the same number of jellybeans. The smallest possible total is then

$$1 + 1 + 2 + 3 + 4 + 5 + 6 + 7 + 8 + 9 = 46$$

3. $\boxed{C}$ The first 4 boxes cost $3 \times 20 + 10 = \$70$. The next 4 boxes also cost \$70. The remaining 3 boxes cost $3 \times 20 = \$60$. Therefore, Jake paid a total of $70 + 70 + 60 = \$200$.

4. $\boxed{C}$ The number 0.75 is equivalent to $\frac{3}{4}$. The minimum of the range is $\frac{3}{4} - \frac{4}{3} = \frac{9}{12} - \frac{16}{12} = -\frac{7}{12}$. The maximum of the range is $\frac{3}{4} + \frac{4}{3} = \frac{9}{12} + \frac{16}{12} = \frac{25}{12}$

5. $\boxed{C}$ $\dfrac{2 - \frac{1}{6}}{1 - \frac{1}{12}} = \dfrac{\frac{12}{6} - \frac{1}{6}}{\frac{12}{12} - \frac{1}{12}} = \dfrac{\frac{11}{6}}{\frac{11}{12}} = \frac{11}{6} \times \frac{12}{11} = 2$

6. $\boxed{D}$ After doing 3 loads of laundry, Martin will have $8.00 - 3 \times 1.25 = \$4.25$ left, which is equivalent to $4.25 \div 0.25 = 17$ quarters.

7. $\boxed{B}$ Lia's bill should have been $113 - 20 = \$93$. Subtracting the fixed fee leaves $93 - 60 = \$33$ for actual travel. Therefore, Lia must have traveled $33 \div 1.50 = 22$ miles.

8. $\boxed{B}$ The chef has enough olive oil for $5\frac{3}{4} \div \frac{2}{3} = 8.625$ pizzas. Since we only want to count whole pizzas, we round down to 8.

9. $\boxed{D}$ When the blank is "minus," the result is $28 - (-2) = 30$. When it's "plus," the result is $28 + (-2) = 26$. When it's "divided by," the result is $28 \div (-2) = -14$. When it's "multiplied by," the result is $28 \times (-2) = -56$. When it's "raised to the power of," the result is $28^{(-2)} = \frac{1}{28^2} = \frac{1}{784}$. The smallest result occurs when the blank is "multiplied by."

10. $\boxed{C}$ The 6 pizzas cost $50.88 - 8.28 = \$42.60$ without the delivery surcharge. That's $42.60 \div 6 = \$7.10$ per pizza. The cost for 8 pizzas is then $8 \times \$7.10 = \$56.80$.

11. $\boxed{D}$ Over the first 4 days, Alistair completes $\frac{3}{20} \times 4 = \frac{12}{20} = \frac{3}{5}$ of the exercise set. That leaves $1 - \frac{3}{5} = \frac{2}{5}$ of the exercise set for the remaining 6 days. At this point, he must complete on average $\frac{2}{5} \div 6 = \frac{2}{5} \times \frac{1}{6} = \frac{1}{15}$ of the entire exercise set each day to finish on time.

Exercise 6: Properties of Numbers

1. $\boxed{C}$ So far, Elizabeth has 6 and 17. We can pick three more for her: 20, 18, and 15. We can't use 16 or 19 because Jamie already has those cards.

$$6 + 17 + 20 + 18 + 15 = 76$$

2. $\boxed{D}$
$$3x + 4x - 14 = 7x - 14 = 7(x - 2)$$

Notice that the result above has a factor of 7. No matter what x is, the result will always be divisible by 7.

3. $\boxed{C}$ We have to test each answer choice out. To be smart about it, start with C and D because they're not even (something that IS divisible by 6 will be even). As it turns out, C is the answer.

4. $\boxed{E}$ The given number is approximately $7.4162^2 \approx 55$, which is between 49 and 64.

5. $\boxed{D}$ Testing each answer choice out, we see that only A, D, and E are divisible by 7. Of those choices, only E is divisible by 6.

6. $\boxed{A}$ $\dfrac{8.1 \times 10^9}{2.6 \times 10^4} = \dfrac{8.1}{2.6} \times \dfrac{10^9}{10^4} \approx 3.11 \times 10^5 \approx 3 \times 10^5$

7. $\boxed{D}$ Dividing by 100 moves the decimal point two places to the left. With this in mind, we can test out each of the answer choices pretty quickly. When we get to $n = -8$, $\dfrac{n}{100} = \dfrac{-8}{100} = -0.08$ and $\dfrac{(n+1)}{100} = \dfrac{-7}{100} = -0.07$. The fact that $-0.08 < -0.0728 < -0.07$ means that $n = -8$ is the answer.

8. $\boxed{B}$ The expression is undefined when the denominator is 0. Setting $9 - y^2 = 0$, we get $y = \pm 3$.

9. $\boxed{C}$
$$\frac{1 \times 2 \times 3 \times \ldots \times 48 \times 49 \times 50}{1 \times 2 \times 3 \times \ldots \times 48 \times 49} = 50$$

Everything cancels out except for the 50 in the numerator.

10. $\boxed{E}$ The first possibility is I, II, and IV being true and III being false. The second possibility is II, III, and IV being true and I being false. In either scenario, IV is true.

11. $\boxed{E}$ You just have to do a little guessing and checking for this question. Adding up 21, 63, 10, and 46 gives a sum with a units digit of 0. Therefore, 82 is the number that was not chosen.

12. $\boxed{C}$ This question is easier than it looks. Every number has 1 and itself as factors so you're just looking for numbers that have only 2 additional factors. Using guess and check, we can actually come up with the following list pretty quickly: 6, 8, 10, 14, 15, 21, 22, 26, 27. There are 9 of these integers.

13. $\boxed{B}$ The factors of 204 are 1, 2, 3, 4, 6, 12, 17, 34, 51, 68, 102, and 204. Notice that the factors come in pairs: 1 and 204, 2 and 102, 3 and 68, etc. We choose the pair that has the smallest difference to be A and B. That pair is 12 and 17, so the difference is 5.

14. $\boxed{A}$ To get the minimum possible value, we want the numerator to be the smallest it can be and the denominator to be the largest it can be. Therefore, we let $a = 11, b = 4$, and $c = 18$, which gives $\frac{ab}{c} = \frac{44}{18} = \frac{22}{9}$.

15. $\boxed{D}$ If the square of x is 8, then x must be either $\sqrt{8} = 2\sqrt{2}$ or $-\sqrt{8} = -2\sqrt{2}$. Both of these values are irrational (cannot be expressed as a fraction of two integers).

Exercise 7: Complex Numbers

1. $\boxed{E}$ $\sqrt{a^2 + b^2} = \sqrt{(-2)^2 + 3^2} = \sqrt{4 + 9} = \sqrt{13}$

2. $\boxed{D}$ The solution $x = 0$ tells us that the equation contains a factor of x. The solutions $x = \pm i$ tell us that the equation contains a factor of $x^2 + 1$. To confirm this, we can plug in $x = i$ and see that $i^2 + 1 = 0$. The result is also 0 when $x = -i$. Therefore, the equation must be $x(x^2 + 1) = 0$.

3. $\boxed{C}$ The product of two complex numbers is a real number only if the two complex numbers are conjugates. The conjugate of $3 - 4i$ is $3 + 4i$. We can multiply them to confirm that the product is 25: $(3 - 4i)(3 + 4i) = 9 + 12i - 12i - 16i^2 = 9 - 16i^2 = 9 + 16 = 25$.

4. $\boxed{D}$ $(3 - i)^2 = (3 - i)(3 - i) = 9 - 3i - 3i + i^2 = 9 + i^2 - 6i = 8 - 6i$

5. $\boxed{B}$ Square both sides and solve for x.

$$\sqrt{x^2 + 9} = 1$$
$$x^2 + 9 = 1$$
$$x^2 = -8$$
$$x = \pm\sqrt{-8} = \pm\sqrt{8}i$$

Therefore, the solution set contains 2 imaginary numbers.

6. $\boxed{B}$ Let x be the other number. Making an equation,

$$x + (5 + 3i) = 10i$$
$$x = -5 + 7i$$

7. $\boxed{A}$

$$2x^2 + 7 = -11$$
$$2x^2 = -18$$
$$x^2 = -9$$
$$x = \pm\sqrt{-9} = \pm(\sqrt{9} \cdot \sqrt{-1}) = \pm 3i$$

8. $\boxed{C}$ $(-2 - i)(5 + 7i) = -10 - 14i - 5i - 7i^2 = (-10 - 7i^2) - 19i = (-10 - 7(-1)) - 19i = -3 - 19i$

9. $\boxed{A}$ $a \pm \sqrt{-4b^2} = a \pm (\sqrt{4b^2} \cdot \sqrt{-1}) = a \pm 2bi$

10. $\boxed{D}$ Multiply both the top and the bottom by the conjugate of the denominator, which is $2 - i$.

$$\frac{(4 - 3i)}{(2 + i)} \cdot \frac{(2 - i)}{(2 - i)} = \frac{8 - 4i - 6i + 3i^2}{4 - 2i + 2i - i^2} = \frac{8 + 3i^2 - 10i}{4 - i^2} = \frac{5 - 10i}{5} = 1 - 2i$$

Exercise 8: Rates

1. $\boxed{C}$ 3 avocados $\times \dfrac{\$4.80}{5 \text{ avocados}} = \$2.88$.

2. $\boxed{B}$ When Greg first started, he averaged $45 \div 10 = 4.5$ minutes per lap. Now he averages $30 \div 12 = 2.5$ minutes per lap. That's an improvement of $4.5 - 2.5 = 2$ minutes per lap.

3. $\boxed{D}$ 30 seconds $\times \dfrac{1 \text{ minute}}{60 \text{ seconds}} \times \dfrac{14 \text{ feet}}{3 \text{ minutes}} \times \dfrac{12 \text{ inches}}{1 \text{ foot}} = 28$ inches

4. $\boxed{C}$ 30 km $\times \dfrac{1 \text{ hour}}{40 \text{ km}} \times \dfrac{60 \text{ minutes}}{1 \text{ hour}} = 45$ minutes

5. $\boxed{A}$ We have to figure out the number of stamps Fred adds to his collection over $40 - 8 = 32$ days:

$$32 \text{ days} \times \frac{5 \text{ stamps}}{2 \text{ days}} = 80 \text{ stamps}$$

Therefore, Fred has $90 + 80 = 170$ stamps at the end of 90 days.

6. $\boxed{D}$ Altogether, everyone drinks $3 \times 3 + 2 = 11$ cups per day. They have enough coffee beans for $11 \times 24 = 264$ cups. If Judy starts drinking three cups a day, they would drink $3 \times 4 = 12$ cups per day. In that case, their supply would last $264 \div 12 = 22$ days.

7. $\boxed{B}$ Kate's document contains $20{,}000 \div 800 = 25$ pages. To make copies, she will have to pay $25 \times \$0.20 = \$5.00$.

8. $\boxed{B}$ Adam took 3 miles $\times \dfrac{1 \text{ hour}}{10 \text{ miles}} \times \dfrac{60 \text{ minutes}}{1 \text{ hour}} = 18$ minutes. Billy took 3 miles $\times \dfrac{1 \text{ hour}}{4 \text{ miles}} \times \dfrac{60 \text{ minutes}}{1 \text{ hour}} = 45$ minutes. Adam arrived at the post office $45 - 18 = 27$ minutes before Billy did. Note that you could've used the formula $d = rt$ to solve this problem instead of conversion factors.

9. $\boxed{D}$ Joey covers the quarter-mile in 0.25 miles $\times \dfrac{1 \text{ hour}}{10 \text{ miles}} \times \dfrac{60 \text{ minutes}}{1 \text{ hour}} = 1.5$ minutes. He covers the half-mile in 0.50 miles $\times \dfrac{1 \text{ hour}}{5 \text{ miles}} \times \dfrac{60 \text{ minutes}}{1 \text{ hour}} = 6$ minutes. So, Joey covers $0.25 + 0.50 = 0.75$ miles in $1.5 + 6 = 7.5$ minutes. Let's call this one "cycle." There are $4 \div 0.75 \approx 5$ cycles that fit in 4 miles, with 0.25 miles left over. That means Joey alternates back-and-forth 5 times, and then runs one more quarter-mile to complete the track. The 5 "cycles" take him $5 \times 7.5 = 37.5$ minutes and the quarter-mile takes him 1.5 minutes. His total time is then $37.5 + 1.5 = 39$ minutes. Note that you could've used the formula $d = rt$ in this problem instead of conversion factors.

10. $\boxed{C}$ Zane's typical routine gets him to school in 1 mile $\times \dfrac{1 \text{ hour}}{4 \text{ miles}} \times \dfrac{60 \text{ minutes}}{1 \text{ hour}} = 15$ minutes. Today he walked the first $\dfrac{1}{2}$ mile in $\dfrac{1}{2}$ mile $\times \dfrac{1 \text{ hour}}{3 \text{ miles}} \times \dfrac{60 \text{ minutes}}{1 \text{ hour}} = 10$ minutes, which leaves him only $15 - 10 = 5$ minutes for the last half-mile. Therefore, he must run at a speed of $\dfrac{1/2 \text{ mile}}{5 \text{ minutes}} \times \dfrac{60 \text{ minutes}}{1 \text{ hour}} = 6 \dfrac{\text{miles}}{\text{hour}}$ to be on time for school. Note that you could've used the formula $d = rt$ to solve this problem instead of conversion factors.

Exercise 9: Ratio & Proportion

1. $\boxed{E}$ Mark surveyed a total of $10 + 31 + 22 + 12 = 75$ customers. Of those customers, 31 wear size-10 shoes. Following this proportion, Mark will buy $\dfrac{31}{75} \times 300 = 124$ size-10 shoes.

2. $\boxed{B}$ x ~~cups of blueberries~~ $\times \dfrac{2 \text{ cups of water}}{5 \text{ cups of ~~blueberries~~}} = \dfrac{2}{5}x$ cups of water

3. $\boxed{B}$ Let the lengths of the 3 sides be $4x, 5x$, and $7x$. Since the perimeter is 112,

$$4x + 5x + 7x = 112$$
$$16x = 112$$
$$x = 7$$

Therefore, the length of the shortest side is $4(7) = 28$.

4. $\boxed{B}$ We only need to use one row from the table. Using the first row,

$$y = kx$$
$$16.68 = k(4.42)$$
$$k = \frac{16.68}{4.42} \approx 3.77$$

Doing the same with any other row will also give a value around 3.80.

5. $\boxed{D}$ It's possible to spot the answer immediately if you "get it" intuitively. If not, there are a lot of ways to do this question. One way is to just solve for x and check the answer choices. Another way is to translate the given equation and manipulate it:

$$x \text{ equals } 78\% \text{ of } 40 \quad \longrightarrow \quad x = \frac{78}{100} \cdot 40 \quad \xrightarrow{\text{Dividing by } 40} \quad \frac{x}{40} = \frac{78}{100}$$

6. $\boxed{B}$ This question is best done by making up numbers. Let $x = 3$ and $y = 2$. If $y = 2$, then $z = 4$. Plugging these values into the expression, we get $\dfrac{2x+y}{y+2z} = \dfrac{2(3)+2}{2+2(4)} = \dfrac{8}{10} = \dfrac{4}{5}$. Note that the result is the same no matter which numbers we initially make up, as long as they follow the specified ratios.

7. $\boxed{B}$ Let the lengths of the sides be $3x, 4x$, and $5x$. As the longest side, the hypotenuse has a length of $5x$ and the legs have lengths $3x$ and $4x$. Since the area is 108,

$$\frac{1}{2}(3x)(4x) = 108$$
$$6x^2 = 108$$
$$x^2 = 18$$
$$x = \sqrt{18} = 3\sqrt{2}$$

The length of the hypotenuse is then $5(3\sqrt{2}) = 15\sqrt{2}$.

8. $\boxed{C}$ Direct variation means that the two variables are on opposite sides of the equation (e.g. $y = kx$). Inverse variation means that the two variables are on the same side of the equation (e.g. $xy = k$). Let D be the demand index of the product. Then

$$wD = k\sqrt{p}$$

$$D = \frac{k\sqrt{p}}{w}$$

9. $\boxed{E}$ Let x be the number of cans of soda Alice drank this month. Then Jimmy drank $\frac{3}{5}x$ cans of soda this month. Making an equation,

$$x = \frac{3}{5}x + 46$$

$$\frac{2}{5}x = 46$$

$$x = 115$$

10. $\boxed{D}$ To feed 24 horses requires $24 \div 8 = 3$ bales of hay, which means there will be $5 - 3 = 2$ bales of hay left over. Two bales of hay can feed $2 \times 15 = 30$ ponies.

11. $\boxed{E}$ Frank's recipe produces $3 + 1 + 16 = 20$ ounces of raspberry spritzer. These 20 ounces contain $40 \times 3 + 10 \times 1 + 0 \times 16 = 130$ calories. Sixty ounces must then contain 3 times the calories: $130 \times 3 = 390$.

12. $\boxed{A}$ Let the electric force between the two particles be f and the distance between them be d. Given that the electric force varies inversely with the square of the distance between the two particles,

$$fd^2 = k \quad \text{for a constant } k$$

When they're 8 centimeters apart, we can make up a number for the electric force f. Let's say it's 10. Solving for k, we get

$$k = fd^2 = (10)(8)^2 = 640$$

Now that we know the value of k, we can solve for the distance when the electric force is half the value we made up (half of 10 is 5).

$$fd^2 = 640$$

$$(5)d^2 = 640$$

$$d^2 = 128$$

$$d = \sqrt{128} = 8\sqrt{2}$$

Note that we didn't have to make up a number for f. We could've done everything the same way algebraically by letting the initial force be f_i and $k = 64f_i$, but I think working with concrete numbers makes it easier. The result is always $8\sqrt{2}$ no matter what number you make up for f.

Exercise 10: Percent

1. $\boxed{C}$ $0.80 \times 84,000 = 67,200$

2. $\boxed{E}$

$$0.60 \times 210 = 0.40x$$
$$126 = 0.40x$$
$$x = 315$$

3. $\boxed{C}$ $180(0.90)(0.85) = \$137.70$

4. $\boxed{E}$ If $x = 0.2y$, then $y = 5x$. Using this result, 125% of $y = 1.25y = 1.25(5x) = 6.25x$. That's 625% of x.

5. $\boxed{A}$ Let the original price of the TV be x. The final price that John pays is $(0.70)(0.80)x = 0.56x$. That's equivalent to a $1 - 0.56 = 0.44 = 44\%$ discount off the original price.

6. $\boxed{D}$ Let the initial number be x. The final number is then $(0.60)(1.30)x = 0.78x$. The final number is 78% of the original number.

7. $\boxed{A}$ Initially, there are $0.60 \times 20 = 12$ ounces of pineapple juice in the drink. After 5 ounces are added, there are $12 + 5 = 17$ ounces of pineapple juice in a drink that is now $20 + 5 = 25$ ounces. That's a percentage of $\dfrac{17}{25} = 0.68 = 68\%$.

8. $\boxed{D}$ Rachel sold $110 \times 0.80 = 88$ chocolate chip cookies and $140 \times 0.40 = 56$ oatmeal cookies for a total of $88 + 56 = 144$ cookies. She started with $110 + 140 = 250$ cookies and her goal is to sell $250 \times 0.70 = 175$ of them. Therefore, she needs to sell $175 - 144 = 31$ more.

9. $\boxed{D}$ Let the cost of a medium pizza be m. Then the cost of a large pizza is $1.40m$ and the cost of a small pizza is $0.80m$. Using the formula for percent change, we calculate the cost of a large pizza to be $\dfrac{1.40m - 0.80m}{0.80m} = \dfrac{0.6m}{0.8m} = \dfrac{3}{4} = 75\%$ greater than the cost of a small pizza.

10. $\boxed{E}$ Store A: $800(1.08)(0.75) = \$648$. Store B: $800(0.75)(1.08) = \$648$. It's the same amount at either store. This should make sense to you intuitively. At Store A, Matt pays a higher sales tax but then gets a higher discount because that discount is applied to the sales tax. At Store B, Matt gets a smaller discount but pays less sales tax because that tax is applied to the discounted price, not the original price.

Exercise 11: Functions

1. $\boxed{C}$ $f(-1) = \dfrac{5((-1)^2 + (-1) - 6)}{(-1) - 2} = \dfrac{5(-6)}{-3} = \dfrac{-30}{-3} = 10$

2. $\boxed{E}$ $f(3) = 9 - (-2)^3 = 9 - (-8) = 17$

3. $\boxed{C}$ Starting from inside the parentheses, $\bigstar(\bigstar 5) = \bigstar(10) = 10 + 3 = 13$

4. $\boxed{B}$ Test out each answer choice. You'll find that $f(-4) = 0$. Therefore, -4 is a zero.

5. $\boxed{D}$

$$6 \circledast 4 = 8 \circledast n$$
$$3(6) - 2(4) = 3(8) - 2n$$
$$10 = 24 - 2n$$
$$-14 = -2n$$
$$n = 7$$

6. $\boxed{C}$ First, $f(2x) = -2(2x) + 3 = -4x + 3$. Then, $f(f(2x)) = f(-4x + 3) = -2(-4x + 3) + 3 = 8x - 6 + 3 = 8x - 3$

7. $\boxed{C}$ We can test out each answer choice with $x = 5$. Answer A gives 10, answer B gives 25, answer C gives 32, answer D gives $\dfrac{2}{5}$, and answer E gives $\sqrt{5} \approx 2.24$. The greatest among these values is 32, answer C.

8. $\boxed{A}$ First, $g(2m) = 3(2m) - 2 = 6m - 2$. Then, $f(g(2m)) = f(6m - 2) = \dfrac{1}{2}(6m - 2) + 1 = (3m - 1) + 1 = 3m$.

9. $\boxed{C}$ First, $f(2) = |2| - 5 = -3$. Then, $f(f(2)) = f(-3) = |-3| - 5 = -2$.

10. $\boxed{A}$ $f^{-1}(2) = -1$ because $f(x)$ gives an output of 2 when $x = -1$.

11. $\boxed{E}$ $g(3) = f(3 - 5) + 4 = f(-2) + 4 = 5 + 4 = 9$.

12. $\boxed{D}$ For $x^2 - y^2$ to be at a maximum, x should be as large as possible (positive or negative) and y should be as small as possible (positive or negative but preferably 0). Therefore, x should be -8 and y should be 0, giving a maximum value of $(-8)^2 - 0^2 = 64$.

13. $\boxed{E}$ The transformation $-f(x)$ reflects the graph across the x-axis. In other words, it flips it upside-down, turning negative y-values positive and positive y-values negative. The graph that shows the correct result is E.

14. $\boxed{C}$ For convenience, let $y = f(x)$. Then, $y = \dfrac{1-2x}{3}$. Swapping x and y, we get $x = \dfrac{1-2y}{3}$. Now we solve for y:

$$x = \frac{1-2y}{3}$$
$$3x = 1 - 2y$$
$$3x - 1 = -2y$$
$$1 - 3x = 2y$$
$$y = \frac{1-3x}{2}$$

This "new" y is $f^{-1}(x)$. So, $f^{-1}(x) = \dfrac{1-3x}{2}$.

15. $\boxed{E}$ $y = g(f(x)) = g(ax+2) = \sqrt{ax+2+4} = \sqrt{ax+6}$. Since the graph passes through $(5, 9)$, we can use this point to solve for a:

$$y = \sqrt{ax+6}$$
$$9 = \sqrt{5a+6}$$
$$81 = 5a + 6$$
$$75 = 5a$$
$$a = 15$$

16. $\boxed{D}$ Remember how functions and their inverses relate to one another? The inputs x (a.k.a domain) to $g^{-1}(x)$ are the outputs of $g(x)$. In other words, the range of $g(x)$ is the domain of $g^{-1}(x)$. So the question boils down to which values can never be the output of $g(x) = 2^x$. Well, 2^x can never be 0 or negative. Therefore, -1 and 0 are not in the domain of $g^{-1}(x)$.

17. $\boxed{D}$ Because the graph of f has 3 "segments" (down, up, down), the least possible degree is 3.

18. $\boxed{C}$ The denominator $x^2 - 9 = (x+3)(x-3)$, and so it's equal to 0 when $x = \pm 3$. Because we can't divide by 0, $g(x)$ is undefined at $x = -3$ and $x = 3$. This gives us 2 vertical asymptotes. To see if there are any horizontal asymptotes, we can graph $g(x)$:

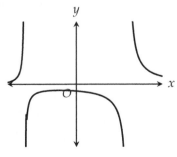

As you can see, there is one horizontal asymptote at $y = 0$.

19. $\boxed{B}$ $y = f(g(x)) = f(x + b) = (x + b)^2 - 3$. We have a couple options here. We can make up a value for b and use our graphing calculator. Or we might realize that since $b > 0$, the graph we're looking for is actually the graph of f shifted b units to the left (you'd have to know your function transformations).

20. $\boxed{D}$ With function transformation questions, we typically have to identify the final graph, but in this question, we're given the final graph $2f(x - 1)$ and we have to figure out the original graph $f(x)$. In other words, we have to work backwards. The fact that $y = 2f(x - 1)$ means that the given graph, relative to f, is shifted to the right by 1 and made narrower by a factor of 2. Therefore, f must be the graph that is 1 unit to the left of the given graph and wider than the given graph. The graph that meets those conditions is D.

21. $\boxed{E}$ Comparing the "peak" points, the graph of g, relative to the graph of f, is shifted to the left by 3 and up by 3. Based on these transformations, we can narrow down our answers to C and E. To decide between them, notice that the graph of g is also narrower, which means the coefficient out in front must be greater than 1. Therefore, $g(x) = 2f(x + 3) + 3$. Make sure to review function transformations if you found this question confusing.

22. $\boxed{D}$ The question is saying that $f(t + 3) = f(t + 1) + 8$. We test out each answer choice to see which function definition makes this equation true. With answer A, for example, we assume $f(x) = x + 10$:

$$f(t + 3) = f(t + 1) + 8$$
$$(t + 3) + 10 = (t + 1) + 10 + 8$$
$$t + 13 = t + 19$$

But because $t + 13$ is not in fact equal to $t + 19$, answer A cannot be the definition of $f(x)$. Getting to answer D, we assume $f(x) = 4x + 6$:

$$f(t + 3) = f(t + 1) + 8$$
$$4(t + 3) + 6 = 4(t + 1) + 6 + 8$$
$$4t + 12 + 6 = 4t + 4 + 6 + 8$$
$$4t + 18 = 4t + 18$$

That worked!

Exercise 12: Lines

1. $\boxed{A}$ When $y = 0$, $0 = 3x + 15$ and $x = -5$. Therefore, -5 is the x-intercept.

2. $\boxed{E}$ $\dfrac{4 - (-2)}{-5 - 4} = \dfrac{6}{-9} = -\dfrac{2}{3}$

3. $\boxed{A}$ When $y = 0$, $x = -6$. Therefore, the line crosses the x-axis at $(-6, 0)$.

4. $\boxed{A}$ When put in slope-intercept form, the given line has equation $y = \dfrac{1}{2}x - 3$. A perpendicular line must then have slope -2. The only answer choice that has a slope of -2 is A.

5. $\boxed{D}$ The line has a positive y-intercept and a negative slope. At $x = 5$, y is less than -5. The only answer choice that meets these conditions is D.

6. $\boxed{E}$ A parallel line will have a slope that's equal to the slope of the graphed line. The slope of the graphed line is $\dfrac{0 - (-6)}{4 - 0} = \dfrac{6}{4} = \dfrac{3}{2}$.

7. $\boxed{D}$ A line that's perpendicular to the y-axis must be a horizontal line. The only horizontal line in the answer choices is D.

8. $\boxed{B}$

$$\frac{8 - k}{k + 5 - 3} = 3$$
$$\frac{8 - k}{k + 2} = 3$$
$$8 - k = 3(k + 2)$$
$$8 - k = 3k + 6$$
$$2 = 4k$$
$$k = \frac{1}{2}$$

9. $\boxed{C}$ When put in slope-intercept form, the given line has equation $y = \dfrac{3}{4}x + \dfrac{5}{4}$. Therefore, its slope is $\dfrac{3}{4}$.

10. $\boxed{C}$ The given line has a y-intercept of 3 (when $x = 0$) and an x-intercept of 5 (when $y = 0$). If you plot these two points and draw a line through them, the line will pass through quadrants I, II, and IV.

11. $\boxed{C}$ Try to visualize the region. Hopefully, you see a triangle:

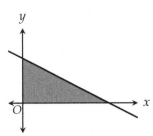

The base of the triangle is the x-intercept, which is 6. The height of the triangle is the y-intercept, which is 3. The area of the triangle is then $\frac{1}{2}bh = \frac{1}{2}(6)(3) = 9$.

12. $\boxed{B}$ The given line has a y-intercept of c. Drawing a rough sketch, we get a triangle with height c.

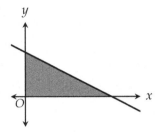

The base of the triangle is the x-intercept of the line, which turns out to be $2c$ (we got this by plugging in $y = 0$ and solving for x). Since the area of the triangle is 36,

$$\frac{1}{2}bh = 36$$
$$\frac{1}{2}(2c)(c) = 36$$
$$c^2 = 36$$
$$c = 6$$

13. $\boxed{B}$ We always get a single line when $a = b$. We always get two intersecting lines when $a \neq b$ (they'll always intersect at the origin). It's impossible to get two distinct parallel lines because the slopes are only equal when $a = b$, and in that case, they're the same line.

Exercise 13: Quadratics

1. $\boxed{B}$ $x^2 + 7x - 30 = (x + 10)(x - 3)$. Therefore, the solution set is $\{-10, 3\}$.

2. $\boxed{C}$ A quadratic with only one real zero must be tangent to the x-axis. Only answer C is tangent to the x-axis.

3. $\boxed{D}$

$$x^2 + 4x - 12 = 9$$
$$x^2 + 4x - 21 = 0$$
$$(x + 7)(x - 3) = 0$$
$$x = -7, 3$$

4. $\boxed{D}$ Based on the solutions, the quadratic must have factors $(x + 3)$ and $(x - 2)$. Putting these factors together, $(x + 3)(x - 2) = x^2 + x - 6$ and we can see that $c = 1$. We could've also done this question by using the sum of the roots property of quadratics.

5. $\boxed{D}$ Based on the equation, the product of the solutions must be -12. Therefore, the other solution is $-12 \div -3 = 4$.

6. $\boxed{B}$ $x = \dfrac{-b \pm \sqrt{b^2 - 4ac}}{2a} = \dfrac{-7 \pm \sqrt{(7)^2 - 4(1)(-5)}}{2(1)}$

7. $\boxed{B}$ The vertex of a parabola with equation $y = a(x - h)^2 + k$ is (h, k). For the parabola in question, its vertex is $(-2, -1)$. Furthermore, it must open upward like a "U" because $a > 0$. Only answer B gives a graph that meets these conditions.

8. $\boxed{C}$ The equation will have no real solutions when the discriminant of the quadratic is less than 0. In this case, the discriminant is $b^2 - 4ac = (-k)^2 - 4(1)(3) = k^2 - 12$. Testing each answer choice, only answer C gives a k such that $k^2 - 12 < 0$.

9. $\boxed{A}$ Based on the equation, the vertex is at $(-3, -2)$, which means the axis of symmetry is $x = -3$. The two x-intercepts are opposite each other, evenly spaced from this line. There are $1 - (-3) = 4$ units from -3 to 1. The other x-intercept must then be 4 units in the opposite direction: $-3 - 4 = -7$.

10. $\boxed{D}$ The graph intercepts the x-axis at -4 and 2, which means $(x + 4)$ and $(x - 2)$ must be factors of the equation. Only answers A and D contain both these factors. To decide between these two options, we can use a point. When $x = 0$, the graph gives a y of about -16. Only answer D does the same (answer A gives $y = -4$ when $x = 0$).

11. $\boxed{C}$ $h = 3t^2 - 24t - 27 = 3(t^2 - 8t - 9) = 3(t - 9)(t + 1)$. Therefore, the missile reaches sea level after 9 seconds.

12. $\boxed{C}$ The x-intercepts of a parabola are always opposite each other, evenly spaced from the axis of symmetry. Since one of the x-intercepts is $(m - \sqrt{3}, 0)$, $\sqrt{3}$ units from the axis of symmetry, the other must be $(m + \sqrt{3}, 0)$.

Exercise 14: Coordinate Geometry

1. $\boxed{B}$ $(8-5, 4-9) = (3, -5)$

2. $\boxed{C}$ The x-coordinate of the midpoint is the average of the x-coordinates of the endpoints: $\dfrac{\frac{3}{2} + \frac{5}{2}}{2} = \dfrac{\frac{8}{2}}{2} = \dfrac{4}{2} = 2$. The y-coordinate of the midpoint is the average of the y-coordinates of the endpoints: $\dfrac{4-6}{2} = \dfrac{-2}{2} = -1$. The midpoint has coordinates $(2, -1)$.

3. $\boxed{D}$ To get from A to A', we have to move 3 units to the right and 2 units down. It's the same from B to B'. Therefore, C' must be 3 units to the right of and 2 units down from $C(3,5)$. That gets us to $(3+3, 5-2) = (6,3)$.

4. $\boxed{A}$ In any parallelogram, opposite sides are parallel and equal in length. Therefore, the two vertices on the left must have the same relative positions with respect to one another as the two vertices on the right. The point $(2,6)$ is 3 units to the right of and 4 units up from $(-1, 2)$. So the coordinates of the vertex P must be 3 units to the right of and 4 units up from $(7,2)$. That gets us to $(7+3, 2+4) = (10, 6)$.

5. $\boxed{C}$ Using the midpoint formula, $\dfrac{1+a}{2} = 3$ and $\dfrac{-12+b}{2} = -8$. Solving for a,

$$\frac{1+a}{2} = 3$$
$$1 + a = 6$$
$$a = 5$$

Solving for b,

$$\frac{-12+b}{2} = -8$$
$$-12 + b = -16$$
$$b = -4$$

Therefore, $a + b = 5 + (-4) = 1$.

6. $\boxed{E}$ Here's what a curve symmetric about the x-axis might look like:

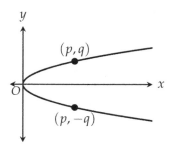

So, the curve must also cross $(p, -q)$, the corresponding point on the other side of the x-axis.

7. $\boxed{A}$ Since $\overline{AC}$ is a horizontal line segment, we can subtract the y-coordinate of A from the y-coordinate of B to get the height: $3 - 1 = 2$.

8. $\boxed{D}$ A good way to picture this is to draw $\overline{OC}$ and perform the rotation on $\overline{OC}$, ignoring the triangle itself.

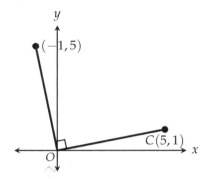

   A well-drawn graph and your intuition are all you need to determine that the new coordinates are $(-1, 5)$. Note that the rotation was about the origin, NOT point A. If the rotation had been about point A, the new coordinates would've been $(1, 5)$.

9. $\boxed{B}$ Use the distance formula to find the distance between the two points:

$$d = \sqrt{(y_2 - y_1)^2 + (x_2 - x_1)^2} = \sqrt{(12 - 4)^2 + (-3 - 6)^2} = \sqrt{8^2 + (-9)^2} = \sqrt{64 + 81} = \sqrt{145} \approx 12$$

   Since 1 coordinate unit represents 20 miles, 12 coordinate units represent $12 \times 20 = 240$ miles.

10. $\boxed{D}$ When a circle circumscribes a right triangle, the hypotenuse is a diameter. Here's one illustration:

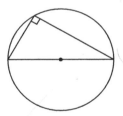

   Therefore, $\overline{BC}$ is a diameter and the center of the circle is at the midpoint of $\overline{BC}$. Using the midpoint formula, $\left(\dfrac{2 + 6}{2}, \dfrac{5 + (-3)}{2} \right) = \left(\dfrac{8}{2}, \dfrac{2}{2} \right) = (4, 1)$.

11. $\boxed{D}$ Point M is $8 - 2 = 6$ units down from the horizontal line $y = 8$. Its reflection, point M', must then be 6 units up from $y = 8$. Therefore, the coordinates of M' are $(-3, 8 + 6) = (-3, 14)$.

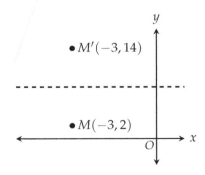

12. $\boxed{A}$ The midpoint of $\overline{AB}$ is $\left(\dfrac{-2+4}{2}, \dfrac{6+8}{2}\right) = (1,7)$. The midpoint of $\overline{CD}$ is $\left(\dfrac{7+5}{2}, \dfrac{5-1}{2}\right) = (6,2)$.

The distance between these two midpoints is

$$\sqrt{(y_2 - y_1)^2 + (x_2 - x_1)^2} = \sqrt{(2-7)^2 + (6-1)^2} = \sqrt{(-5)^2 + (5)^2} = \sqrt{50}$$

13. $\boxed{D}$ Draw a vertical line from A down to $y = x$ and a horizontal line from A to $y = x$ to form a right triangle.

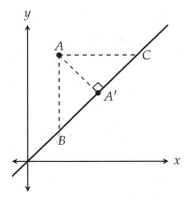

For the purposes of this explanation, we label the intersection points B and C, respectively. Since these points are on the line $y = x$, point B is at $(2,2)$ and point C is at $(7,7)$. Because the triangle is isosceles $(AB = AC = 5)$, point A' is at the midpoint of $\overline{BC}$. Using the midpoint formula to find the coordinates, $\left(\dfrac{2+7}{2}, \dfrac{2+7}{2}\right) = \left(\dfrac{9}{2}, \dfrac{9}{2}\right) = (4.5, 4.5)$.

Exercise 15: Angles

1. $\boxed{C}$ $\angle ADC$ is $180 - 24 - 80 = 76°$. Since angles that form a straight line sum to $180°$, $\angle ADB$ measures $180 - 76 - 40 = 64°$.

2. $\boxed{B}$ Because lines m and n are parallel, $\angle ABC = \angle BCD = 30°$. The value of y is then $180 - 35 - 30 = 115$.

3. $\boxed{E}$ Answer E is the only one that is guaranteed by the properties of parallel lines: g is equal to f, and f and d are same side interior angles, which sum to $180°$. Therefore, g and d must also sum to $180°$.

4. $\boxed{D}$ In a parallelogram, opposite sides are parallel. That means $\overline{AB}$ is parallel to $\overline{CD}$, and $\angle BCD = \angle ABC = 180 - 86 - 34 = 60°$.

5. $\boxed{C}$ $\angle ABD$ is an exterior angle to $\angle A$ and $\angle C$, which means

$$\angle A + \angle C = \angle ABD$$
$$a + 67 = a + b$$
$$67 = b$$

The value of a is then $180 - 67 - 67 = 46°$.

6. $\boxed{E}$ $\angle ABD$ and $\angle ACD$ (answer A) must sum to $90°$ since $\angle BAC$ is a right angle. $\angle ABD$ and $\angle BAD$ (answer B) must sum to $90°$ since $\angle ADB$ is a right angle. $\angle ACD$ and $\angle CAD$ (answer C) must sum to $90°$ since $\angle ADC$ is a right angle. $\angle BAD$ and $\angle CAD$ (answer D) must sum to $90°$ because they form $\angle BAC$, which is a right angle. $\angle BAD$ and $\angle ACD$ (answer E), however, do not necessarily sum to $90°$ because they are not angles from the same right triangle.

7. $\boxed{A}$ Using the properties of parallel lines in conjunction with the fact that the reflected angle is equal to the incoming angle, we can label some angles like so:

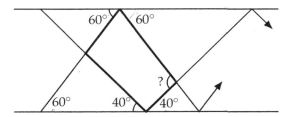

Notice that I've highlighted in bold the quadrilateral in the middle. We're going to use this quadrilateral to find our desired angle. The angle at the top is $180 - 60 - 60 = 60°$. The angle to the left is an exterior angle to the lower left triangle, which means its measure is $60 + 40 = 100°$ (exterior angle theorem). The angle at the bottom is $180 - 40 - 40 = 100°$. Finally, the desired angle has a measure of $360 - 60 - 100 - 100 = 100°$.

8. $\boxed{C}$ Because $\overline{BC}$ and $\overline{DE}$ are parallel, $\angle AFC$ is also $87°$. Note that $\angle AFC$ is an exterior angle to triangle ABF. Therefore,

$$\angle BAF + \angle ABF = \angle AFC$$
$$\angle BAF + 38° = 87°$$
$$\angle BAF = 49°$$

9. $\boxed{A}$ Using $\triangle ABC$, the value of x is $180 - 81 - 40 - 28 = 31$. Using $\triangle ACD$, the value of y is then $180 - 35 - 31 - 28 = 86$.

10. $\boxed{B}$ We draw a line from point C to a point F such that $\overline{CF}$ is parallel to $\overline{AB}$ and $\overline{ED}$.

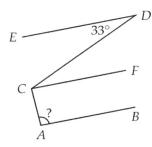

Using the properties of parallel lines, we see that $\angle DCF$ is $33°$ and $\angle ACF$ is $118 - 33 = 85°$. Since $\overline{CF}$ is parallel to $\overline{AB}$, the measure of $\angle CAB$ is $180 - \angle ACF = 180 - 85 = 95°$ (same side interior angles sum to $180°$).

11. $\boxed{C}$ The total number of degrees in an octagon is $180(8 - 2) = 1080°$. Because all angles are equal in a regular polygon, each angle in the octagon is $1080 \div 8 = 135°$. Notice that angles x and y are contained in a pentagon. That pentagon has a total of $180(5 - 2) = 540°$. We can subtract the measures of the three angles at the top from the $540°$ in the pentagon to get the sum of x and y: $540 - 3(135) = 135°$. Notice that we didn't have to find the value of x or the value of y to get the answer.

Exercise 16: Triangles

1. $\boxed{C}$ Using the $45 - 45 - 90$ triangle relationship, we can calculate the length of the hypotenuse, $\overline{BC}$, to be $2\sqrt{2} \cdot \sqrt{2} = 4$.

2. $\boxed{B}$ Using the pythagorean theorem,

$$k^2 + (2k)^2 = h^2$$
$$k^2 + 4k^2 = h^2$$
$$5k^2 = h^2$$
$$h = \sqrt{5k^2} = k\sqrt{5}$$

3. $\boxed{D}$ Using the pythagorean theorem, the hypotenuse has length $\sqrt{6^2 + 10^2} = \sqrt{136} \approx 11.7$, which is between 11 and 12.

4. $\boxed{B}$ $\triangle CDE$ is similar to $\triangle BAE$ because they have corresponding angles that are congruent ($\angle B \cong \angle C$ and $\angle A \cong \angle D$). Therefore,

$$\frac{AB}{CD} = \frac{EB}{CE}$$
$$\frac{AB}{9} = \frac{12}{6}$$
$$AB = 18$$

By the way, $\overline{EB}$ and $\overline{CE}$ are corresponding sides because they're opposite equivalent corresponding angles $\angle A$ and $\angle D$, respectively.

5. $\boxed{D}$ Since $m\angle L > m\angle M$, the side opposite of $\angle L$ is greater than the side opposite $\angle M$. Therefore, $KL < KM$.

6. $\boxed{E}$ Only the side lengths in answer E satisfy the pythagorean theorem ($9^2 + 12^2 = 15^2$).

7. $\boxed{C}$ Using the $30 - 60 - 90$ triangle relationship, $AB = 6$ and $AC = 12$.

8. $\boxed{C}$ Since $\angle B \cong \angle F$, the sides opposite them correspond with each other: $\overline{DE}$ corresponds to $\overline{AC}$. By the same token, $\overline{FE}$ corresponds with $\overline{BC}$ since $\angle A \cong \angle D$. Therefore,

$$\frac{DE}{AC} = \frac{FE}{BC}$$
$$\frac{DE}{7} = \frac{10}{8}$$
$$DE = \frac{10}{8} \cdot 7 = \frac{35}{4} = 8\frac{3}{4}$$

9. $\boxed{B}$ First, draw an initial picture, shown on the left below. The distance between the plant and the shipping center is shown in bold.

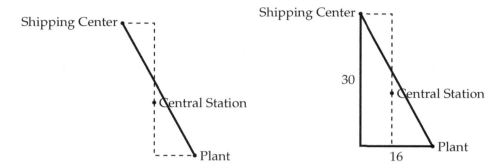

Next, we draw in the large triangle shown in bold on the right above. The base of this triangle is $9 - (-7) = 16$. The height is $18 - (-12) = 30$. We can now use the pythagorean theorem to calculate the distance: $d = \sqrt{16^2 + 30^2} = 34$.

10. $\boxed{E}$ Because their corresponding angles are congruent, $\triangle ABC$ is similar to $\triangle DEC$. Therefore,

$$\frac{CD}{CA} = \frac{DE}{AB}$$
$$\frac{CD}{24} = \frac{14}{18}$$
$$CD = \frac{14}{18} \cdot 24 = \frac{56}{3} = 18\frac{2}{3}$$

11. $\boxed{D}$ The pythagorean theorem says that if $a^2 + b^2 = c^2$, then the triangle is a right triangle. Well, if we extend that logic further, a triangle is acute when $a^2 + b^2 > c^2$. Think about it intuitively. If a triangle is acute, then the "legs" need to be longer relative to the "hypotenuse," which needs to shrink so that the right angle is no longer a right angle but an acute angle. The only answer choice where $a^2 + b^2 > c^2$ is answer D ($7^2 + 8^2 = 113 > 10^2$).

12. $\boxed{B}$ Comparing the hypotenuse of each triangle, the ratio of the sides is 15:9, or 5:3. Under this ratio, the shortest side of the second triangle must be $\frac{3}{5} \times 9 = 5.4$.

13. $\boxed{D}$ Using the $30 - 60 - 90$ triangle relationship, $\overline{AC}$, the hypotenuse, should be twice as long as $\overline{AB}$, the side opposite $30°$. Therefore,

$$5x - 11 = 2(x + 2)$$
$$5x - 11 = 2x + 4$$
$$3x = 15$$
$$x = 5$$

So $\overline{AB}$ has length $5 + 2 = 7$ and $\overline{BC}$, the side opposite $60°$, has length $k = 7\sqrt{3}$.

14. $\boxed{B}$ Because they are both $40 - 50 - 90$ triangles, $\triangle ABC$ is similar to $\triangle DBA$. The sides opposite $40°$ ($\overline{AC}$ and $\overline{AD}$) are corresponding sides, the sides opposite $50°$ ($\overline{AB}$ and $\overline{BD}$) are corresponding sides, and the hypotenuses ($\overline{BC}$ and $\overline{AB}$) are corresponding sides. For any two similar triangles, the ratio of the side lengths is equal to the ratio of the perimeters. Therefore,

$$\frac{AC}{AD} = \frac{AB}{BD} = \frac{BC}{AB} = \frac{\text{Perimeter of } \triangle ABC}{\text{Perimeter of } \triangle DBA}$$

$AB:BD$ is the only one that shows up in the answer choices. Answer B.

15. $\boxed{C}$ Let the legs of $\triangle DEF$ have length 1. Then the legs of $\triangle ABC$ have length 3. Since both triangles are $45 - 45 - 90$, the hypotenuse of $\triangle DEF$ has length $\sqrt{2}$ and the hypotenuse of $\triangle ABC$ has length $3\sqrt{2}$. That's a difference of $3\sqrt{2} - \sqrt{2} = 2\sqrt{2}$ feet.

16. $\boxed{B}$ From the diagram, we have a $30 - 60 - 90$ triangle to work with. Using the relationship, the base is $\dfrac{3}{\sqrt{3}}$ and the hypotenuse, $\overline{WX}$, is $\dfrac{6}{\sqrt{3}}$. Since all four sides of a rhombus are congruent, WZ is also $\dfrac{6}{\sqrt{3}}$. The area is then $bh = \left(\dfrac{6}{\sqrt{3}}\right)(3) = \dfrac{18}{\sqrt{3}} = \dfrac{18}{\sqrt{3}} \times \dfrac{\sqrt{3}}{\sqrt{3}} = \dfrac{18\sqrt{3}}{3} = 6\sqrt{3}$.

17. $\boxed{C}$ First, draw the height and a line from the center of the square base to the front-left corner. These lines form a right triangle as shown in bold below.

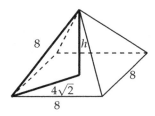

The hypotenuse of the bolded triangle is 8 since the side lengths of the equilateral triangular faces are equivalent to the side length of the square base. We then use the $45 - 45 - 90$ triangle relationship to determine that the diagonal of the square base is $8\sqrt{2}$, which makes the bottom side of the bolded right triangle $8\sqrt{2} \div 2 = 4\sqrt{2}$. Finally, we use the pythagorean theorem to solve for the height of the pyramid:

$h = \sqrt{8^2 - (4\sqrt{2})^2} = \sqrt{64 - 32} = \sqrt{32} = 4\sqrt{2}$.

Exercise 17: Circles

1. $\boxed{D}$ The general equation of a circle is $(x - h)^2 + (y - k)^2 = r^2$, where (h, k) is the center and r is the radius. Therefore, the center is at $(-\sqrt{3}, 2\sqrt{2})$.

2. $\boxed{C}$ Circle A has a radius of x inches and an area of πx^2. Circle B has a radius of $3x$ inches and an area of $\pi(3x)^2 = 9\pi x^2$. The ratio of the areas is then $\pi x^2 : 9\pi x^2 = 1:9$

3. $\boxed{E}$ The general equation of a circle is $(x - h)^2 + (y - k)^2 = r^2$, where (h, k) is the center and r is the radius. Because the radius of the circle is 5, the equation is $(x + 3)^2 + (y - 1)^2 = 25$.

4. $\boxed{E}$ Because the circumference is 16 units, D falls between A and B. If you draw it out, you should get the following:

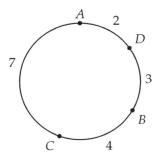

The order of the points is A, D, B, C.

5. $\boxed{D}$ First, find the radius:

$$\pi r^2 = 144\pi$$
$$r^2 = 144$$
$$r = 12$$

The circumference is $2\pi r = 2\pi(12) = 24\pi$. The length of the arc is then $\dfrac{75°}{360°} \times 24\pi = 5\pi$.

6. $\boxed{D}$ Draw the following equilateral triangle. It's equilateral because the two additional segments are both radii and the central angle is $60°$ (one-sixth of the circle), which means all the angles in the triangle are $60°$.

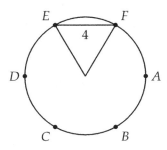

Now that we've proven the radius is 4, the diameter is then $2 \times 4 = 8$.

7. $\boxed{A}$ The full area of the circle is $\pi r^2 = \pi(6)^2 = 36\pi$. The unshaded sector of the circle has an area of $36\pi - 31\pi = 5\pi$, which is $\dfrac{5\pi}{36\pi} = \dfrac{5}{36}$ of the entire circle. Using this proportion, the measure of central angle BAC is $\dfrac{5}{36} \times 360° = 50°$. Because $\overline{AC}$ is a radius that's drawn to a point of tangency, $\angle ACB$ is a right angle. Therefore, the measure of $\angle ABC$ is $180 - 90 - 50 = 40°$.

8. $\boxed{C}$ The full area of the circle is $\pi r^2 = \pi(5)^2 = 25\pi$. The area of the shaded sector is $\dfrac{10\pi}{25\pi} = \dfrac{2}{5}$ of the circle. Therefore, central angle BAC measures $\dfrac{2}{5} \times 360° = 144°$.

9. $\boxed{D}$ The radius of the inner circle is $14 - 5 - 5 = 4$ inches. The area is then $\pi r^2 = \pi(4)^2 = 16\pi$.

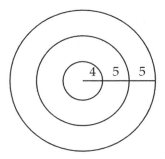

10. $\boxed{B}$ Connect the centers of the circles to form the following triangle:

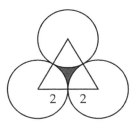

Notice that the triangle is equilateral with side length 4. Each angle of the triangle is then 60°. The perimeter of the shaded region is the sum of the three arc lengths:

$$3\left(\frac{60°}{360°} \times 2\pi(2)\right) = 2\pi$$

11. $\boxed{B}$ A radius that is perpendicular to a chord must bisect that chord. Therefore, $AD = CD = 8$. Notice that $\overline{OA}$ is a radius and must also have a length of 12 inches (same as $\overline{OB}$). Using the pythagorean theorem with right triangle AOD, we get

$$AD^2 + OD^2 = OA^2$$
$$8^2 + OD^2 = 12^2$$
$$64 + OD^2 = 144$$
$$OD^2 = 80$$
$$OD = \sqrt{80} = 4\sqrt{5}$$

12. $\boxed{C}$ First, draw radii to A and B, respectively. Keep in mind these radii meet at right angles with $\overline{AB}$ because $\overline{AB}$ is tangent to both circles. Then draw a line between the centers of the two circles. You might be wondering how you're supposed to know to draw these lines. The answer is experience. What we've drawn isn't anything crazy. Drawing radii (especially to points of tangency) and connecting the centers are common strategies when working with circles.

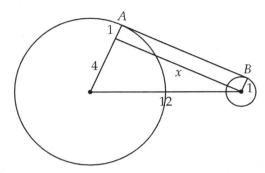

The final key to this problem is to draw a line parallel to $\overline{AB}$ from the center of the smaller circle to the radius of the larger circle (shown above). How did I know to do this? Because a trapezoid isn't easy to work with. With this final line, I now have a rectangle and more importantly a right triangle, which allows me to use the pythagorean theorem. Letting the length of this line be x,

$$4^2 + x^2 = 12^2$$
$$16 + x^2 = 144$$
$$x^2 = 128$$
$$x = \sqrt{128} = 8\sqrt{2}$$

Since x is equivalent to the length of $\overline{AB}$, we've arrived at the answer.

13. $\boxed{C}$ The standard equation of a circle is $(x - h)^2 + (y - k)^2 = r^2$, where (h, k) is the center of the circle and r is its radius. To get the given equation into this standard form, we have to complete the square twice, once for x and once for y:

$$x^2 - 10x + y^2 + 6y - 15 = 0$$
$$[(x - 5)^2 - 25] + y^2 + 6y - 15 = 0$$
$$[(x - 5)^2 - 25] + [(y + 3)^2 - 9] - 15 = 0$$
$$(x - 5)^2 + (y + 3)^2 - 49 = 0$$
$$(x - 5)^2 + (y + 3)^2 = 49$$

Using this equation, we can see that the radius is $\sqrt{49} = 7$. Therefore, the area of the circle is $\pi r^2 = 49\pi$.

Exercise 18: Area & Perimeter

1. $\boxed{A}$ Given the width, the rectangle has two sides of length 6. The two remaining sides must sum to $28 - (6 \times 2) = 16$, and so the length is $16 \div 2 = 8$. The area is then width $\times$ length $= 6 \times 8 = 48$.

2. $\boxed{C}$ Each of the small squares has a side length of $\sqrt{9} = 3$. The square that embodies the shaded area must then have a side length of $3 \times 3 = 9$ (see below) and an area of $9 \times 9 = 81$. The area of the shaded region is half that: $81 \div 2 = 40.5$.

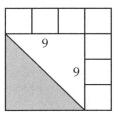

3. $\boxed{E}$ $x + 2(x - 1) + 3(2x + 1) = x + 2x - 2 + 6x + 3 = 9x + 1$

4. $\boxed{A}$ The area of the triangle is $\frac{1}{2} \cdot 16 \cdot 10 = 80$. The area of the rectangle is then $80 \div 5 = 16$.

$$A = bh$$
$$16 = 8h$$
$$2 = h$$

The height is 2.

5. $\boxed{D}$ Using the area of a trapezoid formula is fine, but we'll do this question without it. There are 12 small squares. Each small square has an area of $48 \div 12 = 4$. If we put $\triangle ABC$ and $\triangle DEF$ together, they form 3 small squares with a total area of $3 \cdot 4 = 12$. We then subtract those two triangles from the outer rectangle to get the trapezoid:
$$48 - 12 = 36$$

6. $\boxed{A}$ The area of each square is $54 \div 6 = 9$. The side length of each square is $\sqrt{9} = 3$. There are 14 sides along the perimeter so the perimeter is $14 \times 3 = 42$.

7. $\boxed{D}$ There are 4 faces for each of the 25 cubes in the chain, so there are 100 faces plus the 2 faces on either end. Since each face has a surface area of 1, the surface area of the figure is $100 + 2 = 102$.

8. $\boxed{D}$ If we cut the shaded diamond in half as shown below, we get 6 congruent triangles.

Since the shaded region is made up of two of these triangles, each triangle has an area of $10 \div 2 = 5$. And since $\triangle ABC$ contains 4 of these triangles, its area is $4 \times 5 = 20$.

9. $\boxed{B}$ Subtract the inner square from the outer square to get the total area of the 4 rectangles.

$$\text{Area of 4 rectangles} = 10^2 - 6^2 = 64$$

Since the four rectangles are congruent, the area of the shaded rectangle is $64 \div 4 = 16$.

10. $\boxed{D}$ For percentage problems such as these, one strategy is to make up some numbers. Let the base be 10 and the height also be 10. The area of this triangle is $\frac{1}{2}(10)(10) = 50$. Increasing the base by 30% enlarges it to 13. Increasing the height by 20% enlarges it to 12. The area of this new triangle is then $\frac{1}{2}(13)(12) = 78$.

$$\text{Percent Change} = \frac{\text{New} - \text{Original}}{\text{Original}} \times 100\% = \frac{78 - 50}{50} \times 100\% = \frac{28}{50} \times 100\% = 56\%$$

11. $\boxed{C}$ The base of the triangle is $18 - 11 = 7$. The height is 9. Using the pythagorean theorem, we can calculate the length of the hypotenuse to be $\sqrt{7^2 + 9^2} \approx 11.4$. The perimeter of the trapezoid is then $11 + 9 + 18 + 11.4 = 49.4$, which is closest to 50 in the answer choices.

12. $\boxed{B}$ We need to guess and check the lengths of the sides. Fortunately, this is very easy to do given the numbers we're working with. You should be able to come up with the following:

X	5	7	Y
3	15	21	3
5	25		5
W	5	7	Z

The area of the rectangle in the lower right is $5 \times 7 = 35$, and the area of $WXYZ$ is $15 + 25 + 21 + 35 = 96$.

13. $\boxed{B}$ The area of the rectangle in the upper left is $10 \times 12 = 120$. The area of the rectangle in the lower right is $14 \times 6 = 84$. We can add the areas of these two rectangles and then subtract the area of the unshaded rectangle twice to get the shaded region. We subtract it twice because it's a region shared by both the left and right rectangles. The unshaded rectangle has a base of $12 - 4 = 8$, a height of $6 - 3 = 3$, and an area of $8 \times 3 = 24$. The area of the shaded region is then $120 + 84 - 24 - 24 = 156$.

14. $\boxed{C}$ Notice that because the figure folds into a box, the 7 at the left has to match up with the sides along the top and bottom rectangles:

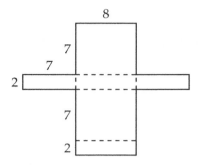

To get the area of the entire figure, add up the big rectangle in the middle (the "body") and the left and right rectangles (the "arms"):

$$((7+2+7+2) \times 8) + (2 \times 7) + (2 \times 7) = 172$$

15. $\boxed{D}$ Given that one side has length 12, the opposite side must also have length 12. The two remaining sides must then sum to $60 - 2(12) = 36$, which means each of them has length $36 \div 2 = 18$. Therefore, the remaining lengths are 12, 18, and 18.

16. $\boxed{D}$ The side lengths of $X, Y,$ and Z are 4, 5, and 4, respectively. The side length of the outer square is $4 + 5 + 4 = 13$. The height of the shaded trapezoid is then $13 - 5 = 8$. The top of the trapezoid has a length of 5. If you don't know the formula for the area of a trapezoid, you can split the trapezoid up into two triangles and a rectangle between them:

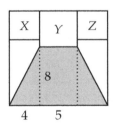

The area is the sum of the three pieces: $\frac{1}{2}(4)(8) + 8(5) + \frac{1}{2}(4)(8) = 72$

17. $\boxed{B}$ Each corner triangle has a base of 4, a height of 4, and an area of $\frac{1}{2} \cdot 4 \cdot 4 = 8$.

$$\begin{aligned} \text{Area of shaded region} &= \text{Area of square} - \text{Area of 4 Unshaded Triangles} \\ &= 12 \times 12 - 4 \times 8 \\ &= 144 - 32 \\ &= 112 \end{aligned}$$

18. $\boxed{B}$ The sum of the lengths of XY and WZ (the two bases of the trapezoid) is the perimeter minus the given sides: $32 - 7 - 6 = 19$. Using the formula for area of a trapezoid,

$$\text{Area of a trapezoid} = \frac{1}{2}(b_1 + b_2)h = \frac{1}{2}(19)(6) = 57$$

19. $\boxed{B}$ If we let one side be x, then the other side is $5x$.

$$A = lw$$
$$200 = (x)(5x)$$
$$200 = 5x^2$$
$$40 = x^2$$
$$x = \sqrt{40} \approx 6.32$$

Answer B is the closest.

20. $\boxed{C}$ We need to find the area of the tennis court. The width is $86 - 4 - 4 = 78$ and the length is $44 - 4 - 4 = 36$, so the area is $78 \times 36 = 2,808$. The owner will need $2808 \div 75 \approx 37.44$ bags of cement, but because only full bags of cement can be bought, the owner will need to round up and buy 38 bags. The total price is then $38 \times 9 = \$342$.

21. $\boxed{D}$ The top side of the trapezoid, b_1, has a length of $4 - (-3) = 7$. The bottom side of the trapezoid, b_2, has a length of $5 - (-5) = 10$. The height of the trapezoid is $2 - (-3) = 5$. Using the formula for the area of a trapezoid, we get

$$\frac{1}{2}(b_1 + b_2)h = \frac{1}{2}(7 + 10)(5) = 42.5$$

22. $\boxed{C}$ Let's draw a picture:

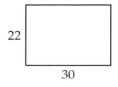

Solution 1: The area of the room is $22 \times 30 = 660$. The "inside" of the room, which is covered with black tiles, has a length of $22 - 2 - 2 = 18$ and a width of $30 - 2 - 2 = 26$. The area of the "inside" is then $18 \times 26 = 468$. The area of the border is what's left over: $660 - 468 = 192$. Now because the area of each tile is $2 \times 2 = 4$, the number of green tiles required for the border is $192 \div 4 = 48$.

Solution 2: Since the green tiles have a side length of 2, there must be 15 tiles along the top and 15 along the bottom. There must also be 11 tiles along the left and 11 along the right. So we can add up all these tiles to get $11 + 11 + 15 + 15 = 52$. However, we double counted the tiles at the four corners. After all, they land on two sides (left-top, left-bottom, right-top, right-bottom), yet we counted them as if they only landed on one side. Therefore, we overcounted by 4. The answer is $52 - 4 = 48$.

23. $\boxed{A}$ The area of $\triangle ABC$ is $\frac{1}{2}(8)(6) = 24$. Using the pythagorean theorem,

$$6^2 + 8^2 = AC^2$$
$$100 = AC^2$$
$$10 = AC$$

Now let AC be the base and BD be the height. Since the area of $\triangle ABC$ is 24,

$$\frac{1}{2}(AC)(BD) = 24$$
$$\frac{1}{2}(10)(BD) = 24$$
$$(5)(BD) = 24$$
$$BD = 4.8$$

Now we can use the pythagorean theorem again with $\triangle ADB$:

$$BD^2 + AD^2 = AB^2$$
$$(4.8)^2 + AD^2 = 6^2$$
$$AD^2 = 6^2 - (4.8)^2$$
$$AD = \sqrt{12.96}$$
$$AD = 3.6$$

24. $\boxed{B}$ Let the length of $\overline{AB}$ be r. To get the area of the shaded region, we need to subtract the area of the small semicircle from the area of the big semicircle.

$$\text{Area of big semicircle} = \frac{1}{2}\pi r^2$$
$$\text{Area of small semicircle} = \frac{1}{2}\pi \left(\frac{r}{2}\right)^2$$

$$\text{Area of shaded region} = \frac{1}{2}\pi r^2 - \frac{1}{2}\pi \left(\frac{r}{2}\right)^2 = \frac{1}{2}\pi r^2 - \frac{1}{8}\pi r^2 = \frac{3}{8}\pi r^2$$

The ratio of the area of the shaded region to the area of the unshaded region (small semicircle) is

$$\frac{3}{8}\pi r^2 : \frac{1}{8}\pi r^2$$

$$3 : 1$$

Exercise 19: Volume

1. $\boxed{C}$ The radius of the cylinder is $8 \div 2 = 4$. The volume is then $\pi r^2 h = \pi(4)^2(7) = 112\pi$.

2. $\boxed{A}$ Because the prism has a square base, $l = w$. Setting up an equation with the volume,

$$lwh = 216$$
$$(w)(w)(8) = 216$$
$$w^2 = 27$$
$$w = \sqrt{27} = 3\sqrt{3}$$

3. $\boxed{A}$ A hemisphere is half a sphere. The volume of the hemisphere is then $\frac{1}{2}\left(\frac{4}{3}\pi r^3\right) = \frac{1}{2}\left(\frac{4}{3}\pi(4)^3\right) \approx$ 134.

4. $\boxed{B}$ Let the side length of the cube be s. Then each face of the cube is a square with area s^2 and because a cube has 6 faces, the surface area is $6s^2$. Solving for s,

$$6s^2 = 384$$
$$s^2 = 64$$
$$s = 8$$

The volume is then $s^3 = 8^3 = 512$.

5. $\boxed{A}$

$$\pi r^2 h = 16$$
$$\pi(x)^2(2) = 16$$
$$\pi x^2 = 8$$
$$x^2 = \frac{8}{\pi}$$
$$x = \sqrt{\frac{8}{\pi}}$$

6. $\boxed{B}$ The radius of the cone is $8 \div 2 = 4$ inches. Setting up an equation with the volume,

$$\frac{1}{3}\pi r^2 h = 250$$
$$\pi r^2 h = 750$$
$$\pi(4)^2 h = 750$$
$$h = \frac{750}{16\pi} \approx 15$$

7. $\boxed{C}$ Set up an equation with the volume and then cube root both sides.

$$(x - 2)^3 = 10$$
$$x - 2 = \sqrt[3]{10}$$
$$x = 2 + \sqrt[3]{10}$$

8. $\boxed{E}$ The container's capacity is its volume: $8 \times 5 \times 4 = 160$ cubic meters. 40% of its capacity is then $0.4 \times 160 = 64$ cubic meters. Since we want to go from full capacity to 40% capacity, $160 - 64 = 96$ cubic meters of water should be drained.

9. $\boxed{B}$ The volume of the first cylinder is $\pi R^2 H$. The volume of the second cylinder is $\pi(2R)^2 \left(\frac{1}{2}H\right) = \pi(4R^2)\left(\frac{1}{2}H\right) = 2\pi R^2 H$. Therefore, the volume of the second cylinder is $2\pi R^2 H - \pi R^2 H = \pi R^2 H$ cubic inches greater than the volume of the first cylinder.

10. $\boxed{B}$ Let the area of the base of Box B be b and the height be h. The area of the base of Box A is then $3b$ and the height is $2h$. The volume of Box B is bh (area of base $\times$ height). The volume of Box A is $(3b)(2h) = 6bh$. Therefore, the volume of Box A is 6 times the volume of Box B.

Exercise 20: Systems of Equations

1. $\boxed{C}$ To eliminate x, we multiply the first equation by 3 and the second equation by 2 and then add the two equations.

$$6x + 15y = 81$$
$$\underline{-6x + 8y = -12}$$
$$23y = 69$$
$$y = 3$$

Plugging this result back into the original first equation,

$$2x + 5y = 27$$
$$2x + 5(3) = 27$$
$$2x + 15 = 27$$
$$2x = 12$$
$$x = 6$$

Finally, $xy = (6)(3) = 18$.

2. $\boxed{B}$ To get rid of the fractions, we multiply the first equation by 4 and get $2x = 3y$. Substituting $3y$ for $2x$ in the second equation,

$$2x + 5y = -16$$
$$3y + 5y = -16$$
$$8y = -16$$
$$y = -2$$

3. $\boxed{D}$ Multiply the second equation by 2 and then add the two equations.

$$2a - b = 6$$
$$\underline{-2a + 4b = 18}$$
$$3b = 24$$
$$b = 8$$

Plugging this back into the first equation,

$$2a - b = 6$$
$$2a - 8 = 6$$
$$2a = 14$$
$$a = 7$$

4. $\boxed{C}$ For there to be an infinite number of solutions, the two equations must be equivalent. First, multiply the second equation by 3 to get matching coefficients for x.

$$3x + 7y = 12$$
$$3x + 3cy = 12$$

Comparing the coefficients for y, $3c = 7$ and $c = \dfrac{7}{3}$.

5. $\boxed{D}$ Since there were a total of 20 questions, $x + y = 20$. Seth received $3x$ points for x correct answers and lost $2y$ points for y incorrect answers. Since he ended up with 40 points, $3x - 2y = 40$.

6. $\boxed{E}$ Let the number of cotton candy bags sold be x and the number of popcorn bags sold be y. Setting up a system of equations,

$$x + y = 140$$
$$5x + 7y = 820$$

To solve for x, we need to eliminate y. To do so, we can multiply the first equation by 7 and then subtract the two equations.

$$7x + 7y = 980$$
$$\underline{5x + 7y = 820}$$
$$2x = 160$$
$$x = 80$$

7. $\boxed{B}$ For there to be an infinite number of solutions, the two equations must be equivalent. First, multiply the first equation by 2 to get matching coefficients for y.

$$2ax - 6y = 12$$
$$8x - 6y = b$$

Comparing the coefficients for x, $2a = 8$ and $a = 4$. Comparing the constants on the right side of the equations, $b = 12$.

8. $\boxed{D}$ Let the number of black-and-white pages be x and the number of color pages be y. Setting up a system of equations,

$$x + y = 50$$
$$1.5x + 2y = 84$$

To solve for x, we need to eliminate y. To do so, we can multiply the first equation by 2 and then subtract the two equations.

$$2x + 2y = 100$$
$$\underline{1.5x + 2y = 84}$$
$$0.5x = 16$$
$$x = 32$$

9. $\boxed{E}$ Don't get confused by the wording of the question. It's simply asking you to find the value of k for which there are an infinite number of solutions to the system. And for there to be an infinite number of solutions, the two equations must be equivalent. First, we multiply the second equation by $10 \div -5 = -2$ to get the coefficients of x and y to match:

$$10x - 6y = k$$
$$-10x - 6y = 12$$

Comparing the constants on the right side of the equations, $k = 12$.

10. $\boxed{B}$ Since there are 25 songs altogether, $x + y = 25$. The x 2-minute songs account for $2x$ minutes and the y 3-minute songs account for $3y$ minutes. Since the playlist runs for a total of 80 minutes, $2x + 3y = 80$.

11. $\boxed{B}$ Let the number of small envelopes be x and the number of large envelopes be y. Setting up a system of equations,

$$x + y = 65$$
$$0.10x + 0.25y = 11$$

To solve for y, we have to eliminate x. Multiply the first equation by 0.10 and then subtract the two equations:

$$0.10x + 0.10y = 6.5$$
$$0.10x + 0.25y = 11$$
$$\overline{}$$
$$-0.15y = -4.5$$
$$y = \frac{-4.5}{-0.15} = 30$$

12. $\boxed{B}$ To eliminate y, we multiply the first equation by 2 and then subtract the two equations,

$$2ax + 2y = 4$$
$$bx + 2y = 1$$
$$\overline{}$$
$$2ax - bx = 3$$
$$(2a - b)x = 3$$
$$x = \frac{3}{2a - b}$$

128

Exercise 21: Inequalities

1. $\boxed{B}$ Dividing by -3 in the last step reverses the sign.

$$4x - 6y < 7x - 9$$
$$-3x - 6y < -9$$
$$-3x < 6y - 9$$
$$x > -2y + 3$$

2. $\boxed{A}$ The medium pizzas will account for $6x$ slices and the large pizzas will account for $8y$ slices. Since 200 slices is the limit, $6x + 8y \leq 200$.

3. $\boxed{E}$ 5 more than the product of 8 and a number b $(5 + 8b)$ is less than $(<)$ 3 times the square of a number a $(3a^2)$. Putting everything together, $5 + 8b < 3a^2$.

4. $\boxed{A}$ Solving the inequality,

$$-4x - 7 \leq 5$$
$$-4x \leq 12$$
$$x \geq -3$$

On the number line, this solution set can be represented by a line that starts from -3 and goes to the right.

5. $\boxed{D}$ After playing Game A and Game B, Susie has $60 - 6 - 12 = 42$ tickets left. The c rounds of Game C will use up $3c$ tickets and the d rounds of Game D will use up $5d$ tickets. Because she cannot exceed her remaining ticket count on Games C and D, $3c + 5d \leq 42$.

6. $\boxed{C}$ Multiply both sides by 10 to get rid of the fractions.

$$\frac{1}{5}y - \frac{1}{2}y < -2$$
$$2y - 5y < -20$$
$$-3y < -20$$
$$y > \frac{20}{3} = 6\frac{2}{3}$$

Therefore, the minimum integer value of y is 7.

7. $\boxed{C}$ Multiply both sides by 3 to get rid of the fraction.

$$\frac{2x - 7}{3} - 1 < 0$$
$$(2x - 7) - 3 < 0$$
$$2x - 10 < 0$$
$$2x < 10$$
$$x < 5$$

8. $\boxed{D}$ The best strategy here is to make up numbers and test out each answer choice. Keep in mind that it's especially important to test negative numbers when there are exponents. If we let $a = 2$ and $b = 1$, we can eliminate choices B and E since they aren't true. If we let $a = -2$ and $b = -1$, we can further eliminate choices A and C, which leaves choice D as the answer.

9. $\boxed{A}$ Since x is always positive and y is always negative, xy must always be negative. That eliminates B, D, and E. The maximum value of xy is -4 (when $x = 2$ and $y = -2$). Therefore, $xy \leq -4$.

10. $\boxed{D}$ When $x - b$ is positive, $|x - b| = x - b$. In this case,

$$|x - b| \leq 4$$
$$x - b \leq 4$$
$$x \leq b + 4$$

When $x - b$ is negative, $|x - b| = -(x - b)$. And in this case,

$$|x - b| \leq 4$$
$$-(x - b) \leq 4$$
$$-x + b \leq 4$$
$$-x \leq 4 - b$$
$$x \geq b - 4$$

So if we put these two cases together, the solution set is $b - 4 \leq x \leq b + 4$. Comparing this with $3 \leq x \leq 11$, we can easily see that $b = 7$.

11. $\boxed{A}$ Translating the 2 conditions into math, we get

$$x = 3 + y$$
$$y > z - 5$$

The first equation gives $y = x - 3$. Substituting this into the second equation,

$$x - 3 > z - 5$$
$$x > z - 2$$

12. $\boxed{D}$ These types of quirky questions are tricky because there aren't any standard procedures we can fall back on. We have to rely on our intuition. If $\sqrt{|x| + 1} \leq 3$, then $|x| + 1 \leq 9$. The maximum possible value of x is then 8 and the minimum possible value of x is -8. All values in between satisfy the inequality. Therefore, $-8 \leq x \leq 8$. Although this explanation makes the question seem easy, it actually requires a lot of thinking. Squaring both sides of an inequality doesn't work the same way as it would for regular equations, even though it seems like that's what we did here. Furthermore, determining the maximum and minimum possible values of x can require some guessing and checking. No one would fault you for taking the brute force approach of testing out each answer choice in this question.

For an illustration of why you shouldn't square both sides of an inequality, let

$$\sqrt{x} \geq -5$$

If we square both sides,

$$x \geq 25$$

But this does not necessarily follow from the original inequality. For example, $x = 1$ satisfies the original inequality but is not greater than or equal to 25.

13. $\boxed{D}$ The inequality $0 \leq x \leq 5$ means the shaded region lies between the vertical lines $x = 0$ and $x = 5$. All answer choices satisfy this requirement. The inequality $5 \leq y \leq 10$ means the shaded region lies between the horizontal lines $y = 5$ and $y = 10$. Only answer choices A and D satisfy this requirement. Lastly, the inequality $y \geq x + 2$ means the shaded region lies above the line $y = x + 2$. Between A and D, only answer D satisfies this requirement.

14. $\boxed{A}$ When $x - 2a$ is positive, $|x - 2a| = x - 2a$. In this case,

$$|x - 2a| \geq 6$$
$$x - 2a \geq 6$$
$$x \geq 2a + 6$$

When $x - 2a$ is negative, $|x - 2a| = -(x - 2a)$. And in this case,

$$|x - 2a| \geq 6$$
$$-(x - 2a) \geq 6$$
$$-x + 2a \geq 6$$
$$-x \geq -2a + 6$$
$$x \leq 2a - 6$$

Putting these two cases together, the solution set is $x \geq 2a + 6$ OR $x \leq 2a - 6$. On the number line, this solution set can be represented by one line that starts from $2a + 6$ and goes to the right and another line that starts from $2a - 6$ and goes to the left.

15. $\boxed{E}$ Given that a and b are positive, line $y = ax + b$ has a positive slope and a positive y-intercept. This eliminates answers B (negative y-intercept), C (negative slope), and D (negative slope). Since $y < ax + b$, the shaded region must lie below the line $y = ax + b$. Therefore, the answer is E.

Exercise 22: Trigonometry

1. $\boxed{A}$ The pythagorean theorem gives $DF = \sqrt{29^2 - 20^2} = 21$. So, $\tan F = \dfrac{\text{opp}}{\text{adj}} = \dfrac{20}{21}$.

2. $\boxed{D}$ The pythagorean theorem gives $XZ = \sqrt{34^2 - 16^2} = 30$. Mentally go through each of the answer choices. Only $\cos Z = \dfrac{30}{34} = \dfrac{15}{17}$.

3. $\boxed{E}$ Let the height of the tree be h.

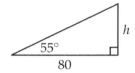

$$\tan 55° = \frac{h}{80}$$

$$h = 80 \tan 55° \approx 80(1.43) \approx 114$$

4. $\boxed{B}$ The minimum possible value of $\sin Z$, no matter what Z represents, is -1. Therefore, the minimum possible value of $\sin bx$ is -1, and the minimum possible value of $a \sin bx - c$ is $a(-1) - c = -a - c$.

5. $\boxed{B}$ Draw two vertical lines from B to $\overline{AD}$ and from C to $\overline{AD}$. Let the points of intersection be E and F, respectively, as shown below.

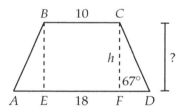

Because the trapezoid is isosceles, $AE = FD$. So, the length of FD is $\dfrac{18 - 10}{2} = 4$. If we let the height of the trapezoid be h,

$$\tan 67° = \frac{CF}{FD}$$

$$\tan 67° = \frac{h}{4}$$

$$h = 4 \tan 67°$$

6. $\boxed{C}$ Because $\csc A = \dfrac{1}{\sin A}$, $\sin A = \dfrac{1}{\csc A} = \dfrac{1}{1.8} = \dfrac{1}{\frac{9}{5}} = \dfrac{5}{9}$.

7. $\boxed{D}$ Let the width of the marsh be w.

$$\cos 37° = \frac{240}{w}$$

$$w\cos 37° = 240$$

$$w = \frac{240}{\cos 37°}$$

8. $\boxed{C}$ Converting the radian measure of the first angle to degrees, $\frac{19}{4}\pi$ radians $\times \dfrac{180°}{\pi \text{ radians}} = 855°$. Now coterminal angles are always a multiple of $360°$ apart, so we can continue to subtract 360 from 855 until we get one of the answer choices: $855 - 360 - 360 = 135°$.

9. $\boxed{C}$ Let the boat's distance from shore be d.

$$\tan 64° = \frac{d}{8}$$

$$d = 8\tan 64°$$

10. $\boxed{B}$ First, draw the triangle. Let the base of the triangle be b.

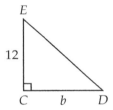

Solving for b,

$$\tan \angle D = \frac{12}{b}$$

$$\frac{4}{5} = \frac{12}{b}$$

$$4b = 60$$

$$b = 15$$

The area of the triangle is then $\frac{1}{2}bh = \frac{1}{2}(15)(12) = 90$.

11. $\boxed{D}$ This is more of an algebra question than a trigonometry one. Just use the given identity.

$$(\sin\theta)^2 = \frac{1-\cos 2\theta}{2}$$

$$\left(-\frac{1}{4}\right)^2 = \frac{1-\cos 2\theta}{2}$$

$$\frac{1}{16} = \frac{1-\cos 2\theta}{2}$$

$$\frac{1}{8} = 1-\cos 2\theta$$

$$\cos 2\theta = 1 - \frac{1}{8} = \frac{7}{8}$$

12. $\boxed{A}$ Relative to the angle in question, we're given the opposite and the hypotenuse. Since sine relates the opposite side and the hypotenuse, the measure of the angle is $\arcsin\left(\dfrac{13}{18}\right)$.

13. $\boxed{A}$ Draw the height h from B straight down to $\overline{AC}$. Solving for h,

$$\sin 38° = \frac{h}{6}$$

$$h = 6\sin 38°$$

The area of the triangle is then $\dfrac{1}{2}bh = \dfrac{1}{2}(12)(6\sin 38°) = 36\sin 38°$.

14. $\boxed{C}$ Since $\sin\theta = \dfrac{3}{5}$, we can draw a right triangle such that the side opposite θ is 3 and the hypotenuse is 5.

The pythagorean theorem gives the length of the third side: $\sqrt{5^2 - 3^2} = 4$ (it's a $3-4-5$ triangle). Using this triangle, $\tan\theta = \dfrac{3}{4}$. Now because we have a positive value of sine, θ could be either in the first quadrant, where tangent is positive, or in the second quadrant, where tangent is negative. Therefore, the possible values of $\tan\theta$ are $-\dfrac{3}{4}$ and $\dfrac{3}{4}$.

15. $\boxed{E}$ The right triangle has a height of 5.2 (the dashed line). Relative to θ, we now have the adjacent side and the hypotenuse. Since cosine relates the adjacent and the hypotenuse, the measure of θ is $\cos^{-1}\left(\dfrac{5.2}{8.4}\right)$.

16. $\boxed{D}$ In the following steps, we don't have to worry about sign changes since the question restricts $\sin x$ and $\tan x$ to positive values. Using the identity $\tan x = \dfrac{\sin x}{\cos x}$,

$$\sin x > \frac{1}{3}\tan x$$
$$\sin x > \frac{1}{3}\cdot\frac{\sin x}{\cos x}$$
$$1 > \frac{1}{3}\cdot\frac{1}{\cos x}$$
$$\cos x > \frac{1}{3}$$

17. $\boxed{D}$ Applying the law of cosines to θ, $7^2 = 6^2 + 11^2 - 2(6)(11)\cos\theta$.

18. $\boxed{B}$

$$\frac{\sin^2 x \cdot \sec x}{\tan x} = \sin^2 x \cdot \sec x \cdot \frac{1}{\tan x} = \sin^2 x \cdot \frac{1}{\cos x}\cdot\frac{1}{\frac{\sin x}{\cos x}} = \sin^2 x \cdot \frac{1}{\cos x}\cdot\frac{\cos x}{\sin x} = \frac{\sin^2 x}{\sin x} = \sin x$$

19. $\boxed{D}$ The maximum of $\sin Z$, no matter what Z represents, is 1 and the minimum is -1. Therefore, the maximum of $2\sin(3x+5)-1$ is $2(1)-1=1$ and the minimum is $2(-1)-1=-3$. The range is then $-3 \le f(x) \le 1$.

20. $\boxed{B}$ The given identity is $\cos(x+y) = \cos x \cos y - \sin x \sin y$. If we let $y = x$, then $\cos(x+x) = \cos 2x = \cos^2 x - \sin^2 x$. With this result, $2\cos^2 x - 2\sin^2 x = 2(\cos^2 x - \sin^2 x) = 2\cos 2x$.

21. $\boxed{E}$ The measure of $\angle G$ is $180 - 22 - 43 = 115°$. Now use the law of sines and cross multiply.

$$\frac{\sin 43°}{40} = \frac{\sin 115°}{FH}$$
$$(FH)(\sin 43°) = 40\sin 115°$$
$$FH = \frac{40\sin 115°}{\sin 43°}$$

Exercise 23: Permutations & Probability

1. $\boxed{B}$ There are $2 + 4 = 6$ fruits that aren't bananas out of a total of $2 + 4 + 9 = 15$ fruits. Therefore, the probability is $\frac{6}{15} = \frac{2}{5}$.

2. $\boxed{D}$ There are 8 choices for the boy and 12 choices for the girl: $8 \times 12 = 96$.

3. $\boxed{E}$ There are n tennis balls out of a total of $10 + 4 + 6 + n = n + 20$ balls. Therefore, the probability is $\frac{n}{n + 20}$.

4. $\boxed{B}$ The number of black pens must be $\frac{3}{5} \times 80 = 48$. The number of blue pens is then $80 - 48 = 32$.

5. $\boxed{D}$ There are 3 choices for the appetizer, 4 choices for the entree, and 4 choices for the dessert: $3 \times 4 \times 4 = 48$ possible dinners.

6. $\boxed{A}$ There are $5 + 23 = 28$ beads in total, 5 of which are green. The probability of drawing the first green bead is $\frac{5}{28}$. Once that green bead is drawn, there are 27 beads left, 4 of which are green. The probability of drawing the second green bead is then $\frac{4}{27}$. Finally, the probability that both beads are green is $\frac{5}{28} \cdot \frac{4}{27}$.

7. $\boxed{B}$ Let the total number of marbles in the bowl be x. Since the probability of choosing a green marble is $\frac{3}{5}$, three-fifths of the marbles in the bowl must be green.

$$\frac{3}{5}x = 18$$
$$3x = 90$$
$$x = 30$$

The number of red marbles is then $30 - 18 = 12$.

8. $\boxed{D}$ We have 6 choices for who we put in the first seat. Once that person is chosen (whoever it is), we have 5 remaining choices for the second seat. Once that person is chosen, we have 4 remaining choices for the third seat, and so on. Multiplying the number of choices we have at each step, $6 \times 5 \times 4 \times 3 \times 2 \times 1 = 720$.

9. $\boxed{A}$ There are 7 numbers in the set. Test each one to see if they satisfy both inequalities (this doesn't take as much time as you might think). The only ones that do are 0, 1, and 2. That's 3 numbers out of 7. Therefore, the probability is $\frac{3}{7}$.

10. $\boxed{C}$ Let x be the number of blue cards that must be removed. Once they're removed, the number of blue cards in the deck decreases to $36 - x$ and the total number of cards in the deck decreases to $24 + 36 - x = 60 - x$. Now we can set up an equation and cross multiply.

$$\frac{36 - x}{60 - x} = \frac{2}{5}$$
$$5(36 - x) = 2(60 - x)$$
$$180 - 5x = 120 - 2x$$
$$-3x = -60$$
$$x = 20$$

11. $\boxed{D}$ We have 3 choices in the first set and 3 choices in the second set, giving $3 \times 3 = 9$ possible pairs of numbers. Of those pairs, only 2 of them sum to 6: 1 and 5, 2 and 4. Therefore, the probability is $\frac{2}{9}$.

Here's another way. The probability of getting a 1 and a 5 is $\frac{1}{3} \times \frac{1}{3} = \frac{1}{9}$. The probability of getting a 2 and a 4 is also $\frac{1}{3} \times \frac{1}{3} = \frac{1}{9}$. Adding up these two cases, we get $\frac{1}{9} + \frac{1}{9} = \frac{2}{9}$.

Exercise 24: Data & Statistics

1. $\boxed{D}$ The row for "Water" gives $56 + 24 = 80$ passengers.

2. $\boxed{D}$ The sum of all 8 numbers is $8 \times 68 = 544$. The sum of the first 6 numbers is $6 \times 65 = 390$. Therefore, the sum of the 7th and 8th numbers must be $544 - 390 = 154$. The average is then $154 \div 2 = 77$.

3. $\boxed{D}$ If you don't know how to read a frequency table, it's easy. There are 3 essays with a word count between 500 and 600, 2 essays with a word count between 601 and 700, and so on. Now, the median word count of 24 essays is the average of the 12th essay and the 13th essay. From the table, the 12th essay has a word count between 801 and 900 and so does the 13th essay. Therefore, the median word count must be between 801 and 900. Only answer D fulfills this condition.

4. $\boxed{E}$ Television represents $\dfrac{45}{30 + 25 + 45 + 15 + 65} = \dfrac{45}{180} = \dfrac{1}{4}$ of the sample. The measure of the central angle is then $\dfrac{1}{4} \times 360° = 90°$.

5. $\boxed{C}$ The 5 original cookies contain a total of $5 \times 9 = 45$ grams of sugar. After the 6th cookie is added, the total sugar content increases to $45 + 18 = 63$ grams. The new average is then $63 \div 6 = 10.5$.

6. $\boxed{D}$ Make an ordered list of the number of moves: $18, 21, 24, 26, 35, 47, 52$. The median is the 4th number, which is 26.

7. $\boxed{D}$ Because White moves first, White always makes one more move than Black in the games where White wins. After all, Black can't make a move after White's checkmating move. In the games where Black wins, White and Black make the same number of moves. Therefore, White made 11 moves in Game 1, 12 moves in Game 2, 26 moves in Game 3, and 18 moves in Game 4. That's a total of $11 + 12 + 26 + 18 = 67$ moves.

8. $\boxed{A}$ From 0 to 30 minutes, John's distance from his house increased. From 30 to 60 minutes, John's distance from his house decreased. Note that he jogged at a constant speed throughout. Of the answer choices, only answer A provides an explanation consistent with the graph.

9. $\boxed{D}$ Draw your own line of best fit.

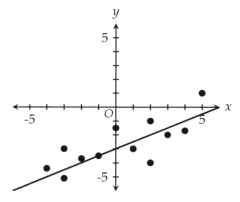

The value of a is equal to the slope of the line, which is positive and less than 1. Only answer D meets these conditions.

10. $\boxed{E}$ Remember that percent change is given by $\dfrac{\text{New} - \text{Previous}}{\text{Previous}} \times 100\%$. In 2005, the studio produced 10 movies. In 2006, the studio produced 15 movies, which is $15 - 10 = 5$ more than the previous year and equivalent to a $\dfrac{5}{10} \times 100\% = 50\%$ increase.

11. $\boxed{D}$ The mode is the number that shows up most often. From the stem-and-leaf plot, the mode of the data set is 53 (appears 3 times).

12. $\boxed{E}$ Answer A is incorrect because the total number of bags represented in the graph is 7, not 11. Answer B is incorrect for the same reason. Answer C is incorrect because it gives a median between 30 and 34. Answer D is incorrect because it gives a median between 25 and 29. Answer E is correct because it gives a median between 35 and 39 and the total number of bags represented in the graph is 11.

13. $\boxed{B}$ Casey had 25 coins in his collection at the end of Month 2 and 38 coins at the end of Month 3. Therefore, he must have added $38 - 25 = 13$ coins in Month 3.

14. $\boxed{E}$ Average speed is total distance over total time: $\dfrac{62 - 8}{4 - 1} = \dfrac{54}{3} = 18$ feet per second.

15. $\boxed{A}$ The median is the 3rd element, $x + 4$. The mean is $\dfrac{x + (x+2) + (x+4) + (x+6) + (x+8)}{5} = \dfrac{5x + 20}{5} = x + 4$, the same as the median. Therefore, the difference between the mean and the median is 0.

16. $\boxed{C}$ Because the mean is 5, the 5 integers in the data set must sum to $5 \times 5 = 25$. The sum of the two missing integers is then $25 - 1 - 2 - 6 = 16$. For the median to be 6, the missing integers must be 7 and 9. Note that they can't be 6 and 10 or 8 and 8 because the integers must all be different. Therefore, the data set is $\{1, 2, 6, 7, 9\}$ and the largest integer is 9.

17. $\boxed{A}$ Remember that when an operation is applied to every number in a data set, it is also implicitly applied to the median. Therefore, we can work backwards by reversing the operations on the median. The median of the second data set is $y - 5$. The median of the original data set is $\dfrac{y - 5}{-1} = -y + 5$.

18. $\boxed{B}$ Because the median is 75 and none of the numbers in the list are equal to 75, 50% of the numbers in the list are less than the median of 75. That's $0.50 \times 60 = 30$ numbers less than 75. Now, $0.20 \times 60 = 12$ of those numbers are less than or equal to 72. Therefore, there must be $30 - 12 = 18$ numbers that are equal to 73 or 74 (greater than 72 but less than 75).

19. $\boxed{A}$ Note that the graphs are of speed versus time. Bob's speed never changes during his routine so his graph should be a horizontal line segment. Amy first bikes at a constant speed but then speeds up. Her graph should be a horizontal line segment followed by a line segment with a positive slope. Only answer A meets our description.

Exercise 25: Logarithms

1. $\boxed{B}$ Let $\log_5\left(\frac{1}{25}\right) = x$. Then by the definition of a log, $5^x = \frac{1}{25}$. Since $\frac{1}{25} = \frac{1}{5^2} = 5^{-2}$, $x = -2$.

2. $\boxed{D}$ By the definition of a log,

$$2^1 = (x-3)$$
$$2+3 = x$$
$$x = 5$$

3. $\boxed{C}$ By the definition of a log, $x = 8^{-\frac{2}{3}} = \frac{1}{8^{\frac{2}{3}}} = \frac{1}{(\sqrt[3]{8})^2} = \frac{1}{(2)^2} = \frac{1}{4}$.

4. $\boxed{B}$ Use the definition of a log to set up the following equation. Then raise both sides to the -1 power.

$$a^{-1} = 5$$
$$(a^{-1})^{-1} = 5^{-1}$$
$$a = \frac{1}{5}$$

5. $\boxed{E}$

$$\log_4 x - \log_4 2 = 3$$
$$\log_4\left(\frac{x}{2}\right) = 3$$
$$\frac{x}{2} = 4^3$$
$$x = 4^3 \cdot 2 = 64 \cdot 2 = 128$$

6. $\boxed{B}$ $\log_3 49 = \log_3 7^2 = 2\log_3 7 = 2k$

7. $\boxed{C}$ By the definition of a log, the equation $x = \log_4 3$ is equivalent to $4^x = 3$. Now, $4^{x+1} = 4^x \cdot 4^1 = 3 \cdot 4 = 12$.

8. $\boxed{C}$ Tackling the right side first, $\log_3 18 - \log_3 2 = \log_3\left(\frac{18}{2}\right) = \log_3 9 = 2$ ($\log_3 9 = 2$ because $3^2 = 9$).

So now we have $\log_7 x = 2$. By the definition of a log, $x = 7^2 = 49$.

9. $\boxed{E}$ We use several laws of logarithms in the following steps. Notice that we cannot combine logs with different bases.

$$\log_2 a - 2\log_5 b + \log_2(3a) = \log_2 a - \log_5(b^2) + \log_2(3a)$$
$$= \log_2(3a^2) - \log_5(b^2)$$

10. $\boxed{D}$ By the definition of a log, $x = \log_2 5$ and $y = \log_2 7$. Therefore, $x + y = \log_2 5 + \log_2 7 = \log_2(5\cdot 7) = \log_2 35$.

Exercise 26: A Mix of Algebra Topics

1. $\boxed{B}$ Let the smaller piece weigh x ounces. Then the larger piece weighs $x + 20$ ounces. Since they weigh 72 ounces in total,

$$
\begin{aligned}
x + (x + 20) &= 72 \\
2x + 20 &= 72 \\
2x &= 52 \\
x &= 26
\end{aligned}
$$

2. $\boxed{A}$ Plugging in $t = 4$, $n = 5,000e^{-0.3(4)} = 5,000(2.72)^{-0.3(4)} \approx 1,505$.

3. $\boxed{E}$ Let the number of red pebbles be r. Then the number of black pebbles is $r + 9$ and the number of purple pebbles is $(r + 9) + 12 = r + 21$. Since there are 84 pebbles in total,

$$
\begin{aligned}
r + (r + 9) + (r + 21) &= 84 \\
3r + 30 &= 84 \\
3r &= 54 \\
r &= 18
\end{aligned}
$$

The number of purple pebbles is then $r + 21 = 18 + 21 = 39$.

4. $\boxed{C}$ We need to isolate r on one side of the given equation.

$$
\begin{aligned}
A &= P(1 + r)^t \\
\frac{A}{P} &= (1 + r)^t \\
\sqrt[t]{\frac{A}{P}} &= 1 + r \\
\sqrt[t]{\frac{A}{P}} - 1 &= r
\end{aligned}
$$

5. $\boxed{B}$ $A = P(1 + r)^t = 10,000(1 + 0.05)^6 \approx \$13,401$.

6. $\boxed{D}$ When the total amount is double the initial deposit, $A = 2P$. Since $r = 0.04$, we can set up the following equation:

$$2P = P(1 + 0.04)^t$$

$$2 = (1.04)^t$$

To solve this equation for t, we have to use the definition of a logarithm:

$$t = \log_{1.04} 2$$

We can now use the change-of-base formula for logarithms to convert this expression to base 10:

$$t = \frac{\log 2}{\log 1.04}$$

Although this type of question has shown up in the past, you will rarely see logs on the ACT.

7. $\boxed{A}$ Let the number of small tee-shirts be x. Then the number of large tee-shirts is $3x$ and the number of medium tee-shirts is $5x$. Since the store sold 720 tee-shirts in total,

$$x + 3x + 5x = 720$$
$$9x = 720$$
$$x = 80$$

8. $\boxed{C}$ If we let the number of essays that Mark grades per semester be m, then the number of essays that Tracy grades per semester is $\frac{5}{2}m$. Since they grade a total of 210 essays each semester,

$$m + \frac{5}{2}m = 210$$
$$2m + 5m = 420$$
$$7m = 420$$
$$m = 60$$

So, Tracy grades $\frac{5}{2}m = \frac{5}{2}(60) = 150$ essays per semester. Over 3 semesters, that's $150 \times 3 = 450$ essays.

9. $\boxed{C}$ Let the number of appetizers sold be x. Then the number of entrees sold is $2x$. The restaurant made $6(2x)$ dollars on the entrees and lost $2x$ dollars on the appetizers. Since net earnings were \$1,200,

$$6(2x) - 2x = 1,200$$
$$12x - 2x = 1,200$$
$$10x = 1,200$$
$$x = 120$$

The number of entrees sold is then $2x = 2(120) = 240$.

10. $\boxed{B}$ The area of the garden is $A = lw = (60 - 2w)w = 60w - 2w^2$. Now for what w is A at a maximum? There are a few ways to figure this out. One way is to graph $A = 60w - 2w^2$ on your calculator with w along the x-axis and A along the y-axis. You should get the following graph.

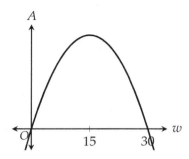

As you can see, the maximum occurs at $w = 15$.

A second way is to realize that $A = 60w - 2w^2$ is a quadratic whose maximum occurs at the midpoint of the two zeros. Factoring the equation gives $A = 60w - 2w^2 = 2w(30 - w)$, of which the two zeros are $w = 0$ and $w = 30$. The midpoint is then $w = 15$.

11. $\boxed{D}$ In maximum/minimum questions like this one, the maximum/minimum always occurs at one of the vertices. In this case, the vertices are $(0,8)$, $(4,3)$, and $(10,0)$. The vertex $(0,8)$ gives $15(0) + 18(8) = 144$ grams of protein. The vertex $(4,3)$ gives $15(4) + 18(3) = 114$ grams of protein. The vertex $(10,0)$ gives $15(10) + 18(0) = 150$ grams of protein. Comparing these values, we can see that the maximum possible amount of protein is 150 grams.

Exercise 27: Miscellaneous Topics I

1. $\boxed{B}$ List the terms out: $7, 11, 15, 19, 23$. The 5th term is 23.

2. $\boxed{A}$ The common ratio of the sequence is $\dfrac{-3}{-9} = \dfrac{1}{3}$. The first term is then $-9 \div \dfrac{1}{3} = -27$.

3. $\boxed{E}$ The common ratio of the sequence is $\dfrac{12}{9} = \dfrac{4}{3}$. The 4th term is then $16 \times \dfrac{4}{3} = \dfrac{64}{3}$.

4. $\boxed{D}$ If we subtract out the first brick, then the length of the remaining row must be a multiple of 9. Now we have to test each answer choice. For answer A, $500 - 8 = 492$, which is not a multiple of 9. For answer B, $501 - 8 = 493$, which is not a multiple of 9. For answer C, $502 - 8 = 494$, which is not a multiple of 9. For answer D, $503 - 8 = 495$, which IS a multiple of 9.

5. $\boxed{C}$ Guess and check. There's only so many combinations of X and Y such that $X + Y = 10$. Eventually you'll find that when $X = 7$ and $Y = 3$, $73 - 37 = 36$. Therefore, the product of X and Y is $7 \cdot 3 = 21$.

6. $\boxed{C}$ Since 44 people had bought both coffee and tea, $98 - 44 = 54$ people had bought only coffee and $76 - 44 = 32$ people had bought only tea. The number of people who had bought at least tea or coffee is then $54 + 32 + 44 = 130$. Therefore, the number of people who had bought neither is $150 - 130 = 20$.

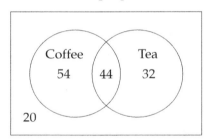

7. $\boxed{D}$ The difference between the 10th term and the 5th term is $13 - 7 = 6$, and since there are $10 - 5 = 5$ steps between them, the common difference of the sequence must be $\dfrac{6}{5} = 1.2$. Therefore, the 4th term is $7 - 1.2 = 5.8$, the 3rd term is $5.8 - 1.2 = 4.6$, the 2nd term is $4.6 - 1.2 = 3.4$, and the 1st term is $3.4 - 1.2 = 2.2$. The sum of the first 3 terms is then $2.2 + 3.4 + 4.6 = 10.2$.

8. $\boxed{C}$ The smallest possible number for the first ticket is 1. The smallest possible number for the second ticket is 2. The smallest possible number for the third ticket is 4 because 3 is the sum of 1 and 2. The smallest possible number for the fourth ticket is 8 because 5 is $1 + 4$, 6 is $2 + 4$, and 7 is $1 + 2 + 4$. If you haven't noticed the pattern, the next ticket number is just the next multiple of 2 (the next ticket number is also 1 more than the sum of all the ticket numbers that precede it). Listing the numbers out,

$$1, 2, 4, 8, 16, 32$$

The smallest possible number for the sixth ticket is 32.

9. $\boxed{B}$ $\dfrac{15 + 37 + 29}{180} = \dfrac{81}{180} = 0.45 = 45\%$

10. $\boxed{B}$ We get each previous term by dividing by 2 and then subtracting 4. The 2nd term is $(48 \div 2) - 4 = 20$. The 1st term is $(20 \div 2) - 4 = 6$.

11. $\boxed{A}$ Let S represent the sum of the series. Then

$$S = \frac{a}{1-r}$$
$$96 = \frac{a}{1-0.25}$$
$$a = 96(1-0.25) = 72$$

Since the first term is 72, the 3rd term must be $72(0.25)(0.25) = 4.5$.

12. $\boxed{B}$ Notice that the numbers at the end of each row are the squares of their respective row numbers. For example, the 3rd row ends with the number 9. The 14th row must end with the number $14^2 = 196$. The 15th row must then start with the number 197.

13. $\boxed{E}$ One level requires 1 triangle. Two levels require 4 triangles. Three levels require 9 triangles. See the pattern? n levels require n^2 triangles. Therefore, 11 levels require $11^2 = 121$ triangles.

Exercise 28: Miscellaneous Topics II

1. $\boxed{A}$ The trapezoid is not symmetrical across the x-axis.

2. $\boxed{B}$ $\begin{bmatrix} a & b \\ c & d \end{bmatrix} + \begin{bmatrix} -a & b \\ 0 & 1 \end{bmatrix} = \begin{bmatrix} a-a & b+b \\ c+0 & d+1 \end{bmatrix} = \begin{bmatrix} 0 & 2b \\ c & d+1 \end{bmatrix}$

3. $\boxed{D}$ If Carl's tie was on display, then it cost more than 50 dollars.

4. $\boxed{B}$ $B = \begin{bmatrix} 4 & 2 \\ -1 & 8 \end{bmatrix} - A = \begin{bmatrix} 4 & 2 \\ -1 & 8 \end{bmatrix} - \begin{bmatrix} 6 & -3 \\ 1 & 1 \end{bmatrix} = \begin{bmatrix} 4-6 & 2-(-3) \\ -1-1 & 8-1 \end{bmatrix} = \begin{bmatrix} -2 & 5 \\ -2 & 7 \end{bmatrix}$

5. $\boxed{B}$ Put one marble on each vertex and one marble on each side. This scenario uses the least number of marbles: 12.

6. $\boxed{D}$ Each corner consists of 3 right angles. Because there are 8 corners, there are $8 \times 3 = 24$ right angles.

7. $\boxed{D}$ There are 4 rectangles that consist of 1 tile, 3 rectangles that consist of 2 tiles, 2 rectangles that consist of 3 tiles, and 1 rectangle that consists of all 4 tiles. That's a total of $4 + 3 + 2 + 1 = 10$ rectangles.

8. $\boxed{E}$ We can get a point if the plane just intersects the tip of the cone. We can get a line if the plane just touches the side of the cone along the slant. We can get a circle if the plane cuts through the entire base of the cone. We can get a triangle if the plane intersects the cone straight down from the tip, perpendicular to the center of the base. We cannot get an intersection in the shape of a rectangle.

9. $\boxed{A}$ Using the determinant to set up an equation,

$$x(x+4) - (3)(5) = 6$$
$$x^2 + 4x - 15 = 6$$
$$x^2 + 4x - 21 = 0$$
$$(x+7)(x-3) = 0$$
$$x = -7, 3$$

10. $\boxed{B}$ The only logical equivalent is the contrapositive: "If the event is not sold out, then the box office is not closed."

11. $\boxed{E}$ The standard equation of an ellipse is $\dfrac{(x-h)^2}{a^2} + \dfrac{(y-k)^2}{b^2} = 1$, where (h,k) is the center, a is the "horizontal radius," and b is the "vertical radius." The graph in question is a "fat" ellipse with a center at $(5, -3)$, a horizontal radius of 5, and a vertical radius of 2. Therefore, the equation of the graph is $\dfrac{(x-5)^2}{25} + \dfrac{(y+3)^2}{4} = 1$.

12. $\boxed{D}$ Matrix X is a 2×2 matrix. For XY to be defined, the number of rows in matrix Y must be equal to the number of columns in matrix X. Since matrix X has 2 columns, matrix Y must have 2 rows. Because choice D has 3 rows, it cannot be matrix Y.

13. $\boxed{A}$ From the matrix equation, we get the following system of equations:

$$x - 5 = y$$

$$7 + \frac{x}{3} = y$$

Substituting y from the first equation into the second,

$$7 + \frac{x}{3} = x - 5$$

$$21 + x = 3x - 15$$

$$-2x = -36$$

$$x = 18$$

Plugging this value into the first equation, y is then $18 - 5 = 13$.

14. $\boxed{B}$ The standard equation of an ellipse is $\dfrac{(x - h)^2}{a^2} + \dfrac{(y - k)^2}{b^2} = 1$, where (h, k) is the center, a is the "horizontal radius," and b is the "vertical radius." The graph in question is a "skinny" ellipse with a center at $(0,0)$. Because it's a "skinny" ellipse, the vertical radius is longer than the horizontal radius ($b^2 > a^2$). Only choice B gives an equation of an ellipse with $b^2 > a^2$ ($25 > 9$).

Made in United States
North Haven, CT
28 August 2022

23379395R00083